A Sense

of Ireland

General Organising Committee

Cyril Barrett	Dept of Philosophy, Warwick University
Roger Cole	*In Dublin* magazine
Sean Corcoran	Folk Music Archivist, Queen's University, Belfast
Gerald Davis	Jazz Producer, Livia Records
Seamus Deane	Dept of English, University College, Dublin
Ambrose Donohue	Traditional Irish Music Promotor
Joe Dowling	Artistic Director, Abbey Theatre
Yvonne Farrell	Dept of Architecture, University College Dublin
Desmond Guinness	Irish Georgian Society
Hilary Kennedy	Director *The Honest Ulsterman*
Raymond Kyne	President, Society of Designers in Ireland
Sean MacReamoinn	Head of External Affairs, Radio Telefis Eireann
John Meagher	Designer, ROSC
Dermot Moran	Administrator, The Irish Writers Co-op
George Morrison	Film Archivist
Brendan Mulkere	Lecturer, Traditional Irish Music
Mary Mullin	Information Officer, Society of Industrial Arts and Designers
Pat O'Kelly	Chairman, Music Association of Ireland
John Osman	Director, Gallery of Photography, Dublin
Nigel Rolfe	School of Sculpture, National College of Art and Design, Dublin
Gabriel Rosenstock	Broadcaster, Radio Telefis Eireann Editor, Publications Branch, Dept of Education
Jim Sheridan	Chairman, Projects Arts Centre
Frank Sutton	Director, Crafts Council of Ireland
Gerald Tyler	Kilkenny Design Workshop
Dorothy Walker	Visual Arts Critic
James White	Director, National Gallery of Ireland Chairman, Arts Council of Ireland
James Wickham	Dept of Sociology, Trinity College, Dublin

Northern Ireland Advisory Committee

John Fairleigh	Chairman, Drama Advisory Committee, Arts Council of N.I.
David Hammond	Producer, British Broadcasting Corporation, Northern Ireland
Ted Hickey	Curator, Ulster Museum
Declan McGonigal	Director, Orchard Gallery, Derry
Havelock Nelson	Musical Director of Studio Opera Group, Northern Ireland
Frank Ormsby	Editor, *The Honest Ulsterman*

Series Organisers

Exhibitions
Mimi Behncke

Concerts
Dinah Molloy

Traditional Music
P J Curtis

Literature
Andrew Carpenter
Peter Fallon

Film
Kevin Rockett

Seminars
Gerry Sullivan
Milo Rockett

Rock
Frank Murray

Graphic Designers

Richard Eckersley
Peggy McConnell
Kilkenny Design
Workshops

Staff

Programme Director
John Stephenson

Dublin

Director
Philippa Kidd

Assistant
Tara Johnston

Press Officer
Paddy Woodworth

Sponsorship
Co-ordinator
Robert Stephenson

Freight/Insurance
Mimi Behncke

Programmes/Catalogues
Siobhan McHugh

Travel/Accommodation
Marian Smyth

Secretary
Geraldine Reynolds

London

Director
Brigid Roden

Assistant
Jane Travers

Public Relations
Helen Anderson/
Jacqueline Richardson
Cromwell Assocs

Distribution
Helena Fedorec

Published in 1980 by
A Sense of Ireland Ltd
22 Wicklow St, Dublin

Ireland House
150 New Bond St, London W1

© A Sense of Ireland Ltd 1980
ISBN 0 950 6831 0 8
All rights reserved

Catalogue editor: Simon Oliver
Assistant editor: Siobhan McHugh
Designed by Richard Eckersley
Kilkenny Design Workshops
Printed by Iona Print Ltd, Dublin

The contents of this catalogue
are a free and fanciful
commentary on the arts in
Ireland in 1980; loosely
related to the various events
in *A Sense of Ireland*

10 December, 1979

Two years ago the idea for a season of the Arts of Ireland, North and South, was raised within the Institute of Contemporary Arts. Since that first seed was sown the event has grown into one of the most remarkable festivals of contemporary Irish art and culture ever presented.

A Sense of Ireland includes over ninety events in theatre, music, literature, the visual arts, film, crafts, dance, photography, architecture and archaeology. As well as the events to be presented at the Institute of Contemporary Arts, over forty other venues, ranging from national institutions to local halls, will be hosts to various aspects of the Festival.

Such an array cannot fail to convey a comprehensive idea of Ireland and the Irish today. It is particularly welcome, therefore, that this manifestation should take place in London. This city is not only a great international cultural centre, but is also the capital of a people who are Ireland's closest neighbours. The Festival, in which Irish artists from both North and South will participate, is intended to increase understanding and friendship between the people of these islands.

It is my pleasure to welcome a Sense of Ireland to London, to wish it well and to congratulate all those who have worked so hard for its success.

Eamon Kennedy

Ambassador

Sponsors

The following companies and organisations, by contributing so generously to A Sense of Ireland, have not only enabled this festival to be so comprehensive, but have also paved the way for much-needed private sector support for the Irish Arts in general. Their sponsorship is greatly appreciated.

List of Sponsors
as at 7 December 1979

Aer Lingus
Allied Irish Banks
Asahi Pentax
Bank of Ireland
B + I Line
Bord Bainne/Kerrygold
Bord Fáilte/Irish Tourist Board
Bord na Móna/Irish Peat
Development Authority
Bord na Gaeilge
British Airways
CBF/Irish Livestock and Meat
Marketing Board
Córas Tráchtála/
Irish Export Board
Guinness Ireland Ltd
Industrial Development
Authority
Insurance Corporation
of Ireland Ltd
Irish Life Assurance
Company Ltd
Irish Shell Ltd
Irish Shipping Ltd
Kilkenny Design Workshops
Lep (Ireland) Ltd
London Tara Hotel
Northern Ireland Tourist Board
P J Carroll & Company Ltd
Radio Telefis Eireann
Sealink (British Rail)
Trust House Forte (Ireland)
Waterford Crystal

Faoi Bhráid Thrí Phobal

Trí phobal, mar mheasaimid, atá romhainn agus an Tóstal mór so d'ealaíona Éireann á chur ar bun againn i Londain. Muintir Shasana sa chéad áit, ós ina bpríomhchathair ársa féin atáimid. Comharsana leis na cianta sinn, agus, bíodh nár ghrámhar ár gcaidreamh i gcónaí, tá suim againn ina chéile ariamh. Tá comharsanacht chultúra eadrainn leis, ach braithimid gur mó an cur amach atá againne ar a saoithiúlacht siúd ná a bhfuil acusan ar ár ndúchas féin. Ní féidir le féile mar seo préamhacha an dúchais sin, ná an ithir ina bhfásaid, a thabhairt anall lena gcur ina luí ar an muintir abhus. Ach is féidir bláthú iolartha ilghnéitheach an dúchais a nochtadh dóibh le taispeántais agus léiriúcháin de gach saghas, idir dhrámaíocht agus cheol agus fhilíocht agus phéintéireacht agus cheirdne — agus a lán eile.

Creidimid go mbainfidh ár gcomharsana taithneamh as an méid sin, agus go méadóidh dá réir ar an dtuiscint atá acu orainn. Tá taithí acu, ar ndó, ar réimsí áirithe dár ndéantús ealaíne, agus ar a saothar siúd, ach go háirithe, a bhain amach máistreacht ar chearda na drámaíochta, na filíochta agus na huirscealaíochta sa teanga Bhéarla. Ach tá réimsí eile ann ar tais a dtreoir orthu: tá súil againn go raghaidh an fhéile seo chun leighis an scéil.

Mar an gcéanna, dar linn, i gcás an dara pobal ar a bhfuil ár n-aghaidh. An pobal so atáimid a rá baineann sé leis an Londain atá, ní hamháin ina príomhchathair náisiúnta ach, dá n-abraimis é, ina metropolis domhanda. Bíonn sráideanna na ceannchathrach so breac le fir agus mná as gach aon chearn den chruinne, agus a bhfuil a ndúchas préamhaithe i ngach aon chine dár cruthaíodh. Is geal linn seasamh i lár an aonaigh mhóir idirnáisiúnta so,

agus is le mórtas a léirímid ár ndéantus dóibh. Teagmháil thairbheach í seo, ó thaobh na dtaobhann. Tá sé ráite gur maith an scathán súil charad: is iliomad scathán maisea a bheidh ar fáil dúinn le linn na féile seo, agus chífimid níos mó agus níos soiléire ná riamh. Is trathúil an ócáid í, gan aon agó, ag ár n-aos ealaíne, idir lucht cumtha agus lucht reice araon, bheith ar aonach chomh héagsúil ilchineálach is atá sé seo. Éire i measc na náisiún, gan amhras, agus brí úr san abairt.

Ach más ar náisiún ar leith a dhírimid áird anois ní tógfar orainn é. Ár muintir féin abhus atáimid a rá, pé acu ó inné nó le blianta fada a gcuairt nó a n-imirce, pé acu in Éirinn a rugadh iad nó abhus — agus a n-aithreacha féin agus glúnta rompu — ach gur de shliocht Gael iad. Cleachtann cuid éigin acu ár dteanga i gcónaí, cuid mhór eile a chlaíonn le ceol agus cluichí a ndúchais: buailfimid leosan go minic ar an aonach agus slánóimid ár gcaid-reamh. Ach is chuchu atáimid go speisialta, sliocht na ndeoraithe a fágadh gan seilbh a n-oidhreachta, agus bheirimid ár ndéantús dóibhsin mar chúiteamh agus mar chomhartha athmhuintearais. Táimid i ndóchas go dtiúrfaidh siad éisteacht dúinn agus go bhfáilteoidh siad roimh ár dtíolacadh.

Seasaimid, mar sin, ós comhair na dtrí bpobal agus beannaímid dóibh. Gura chun chothú na comhthuisceana eadrainn uile, chun dlúthú ár gcaradais agus ár gcur-le-chéile, agus chun taithnimh agus aoibhnis do chách, ár gconaí inbhur measc!

Seán MacRéamoinn

IRISH.

SCENE—*Cottage in West of Ireland during a rain-storm.*

Tourist. "WHY DON'T YOU MEND THOSE BIG HOLES IN THE ROOF?"

Pat. "WUD YOUR HONOUR HAVE ME GO OUT AN' MEND IT IN ALL THIS RAIN?"

Tourist. "NO. BUT YOU COULD DO IT WHEN IT IS FINE."

Pat. "SHURE, YOUR HONOUR, THERE'S NO NEED TO DO IT THIN!"

Introduction

In 1960 when my father brought his family back from emigration in England to start his own business at home in Ireland I was aged almost ten. I remember my first weeks in school in Dublin as a trial. To my fellows I was English. This meant that I was the object of their resentment, expressed in malicious taunting — but with a strain of deference, even of awe. Although these schoolboys wanted to hurt, they wanted more to be friends. Other new boys remained outsiders long after their easy acceptance, yet I was quickly to become an insider, 'a status friend'. After all I was English and this implied superiority. As every Irish child knew the English were monstrous giants who had straddled our land for centuries: the cause of hardship and suffering for our people. But they couldn't altogether be rejected. The Irish spoke their language and mirrored their social habits. The alternative cultural identity which might have enabled the Irish to recognise themselves and establish a self-esteem based on a distinct Irishness did not exist (who ever said "Irish is beautiful"?). By the time our sling-wielding heroes had felled the giant all we could do was apply the same defensive methods in restoring our culture as the English had in suppressing it, with equal success. The gaelic resurgence of the turn of the century had become a Kultur-rump by the sixties, and all other cultural expressions had been palsied.

So my new school fellows had nothing positive of which they were sure and proud, and with which they could challenge or convert me. The first skirmishes had been a probing courtship. The desire to be a peer of one's old master is not a new one and has reduced most of the Irish to being 'Castle Catholics' and Unionists. All this even was three years before the Beatles and all that, which has further re-inforced this process.

One irony in considering the impoverished Gheist of the Irish people is the realisation that in general the English, whose state was instrumental in causing this, tend to have a stronger view of the Irish than we do of ourselves. The paradox is that although this view is almost completely erroneous it is one of the prime moulders of Irish self-awareness.

I grew up in London and Leeds under the shadow of the 50's bombing campaign by the IRA. At some stage, every Irish immigrant in England has had the experience of being called "an Irish pig", and of being an object of fear, hate or derision at least indirectly, but often personally. The tragedy of this situation is primarily England's. As a child I reacted with tears and fierce and floundering pride. The shame was my accuser's, but it drove me into myself. The Irish in Britain have internalised this kind of thing by retreating into various mental ghettoes across a spectrum from the chameleon to the strident 'paddy', all of them artificial. Layers of disguise became our survival mechanism, but the warps thus created do us more harm. We define ourselves in reaction. I remember such moments as my parents panic-stricken attempts to dump an old pair of Wellingtons which co-incidentally bore the inscription of the fairly common name of a wanted IRA man. John Cleese couldn't have done better. But there was little humour in this situation.

The fear is mutual. There was also the English couple who watched for weeks as their winter coal supply disappeared, rather than inform us that we were going to the wrong bunker. At least the fun of that emerged, and they became friends, like so many others who were, and are, good friends. England's history has produced a people who are at once the most tolerant and intolerant. This world-wise people have developed two mutually contradictory views of the Irish, both of which they hold at any given time to be true. On the one hand we are lazy, primitive, drunken, stupid and violent. On the other we are witty, cultured, gregarious, charming and lovable. In this mythology we are limited to being oafish ogres or spritely elves. Even personal acquaintance doesn't totally eliminate the general myths, as they remain an underlying view among our English friends and colleagues which slip out in unguarded moments; and also sadly because too many of us resort to these myths ourselves.

In the last twenty years, and ten years in particular, Ireland has been transformed, South and North, more radically than any other country in Europe. The South has moved from a conservative and insular small farmer base with massive emigration, beyond the first stages of industrialisation and modernisation, to establishing itself as a rapidly developing Western European mixed economy. New industries with an emphasis on light electronics, progressive agri-business, increasing population and decreasing emigration, extensive tourism, service and communications industries — all combine in a relatively stable social and political system. This is not to say that there are not problems and contradictions, such as acute areas of poverty, cultural and personal dislocation, blighted urban spread — at once prompted and mitigated by rampant acquisitiveness. It does however serve to demonstrate that Ireland and the Irish are a place and a people like many others, and that those qualities that do mark us apart must be explained as much in this new context as in our past history, rather than in the historically unreal stereotypes still so prevalent.

The North also has changed dramatically. The stable sectarian statelet with its proud industrial and agricultural base has disintegrated. Moribund industry, increasingly disadvantaged farmers, physical decay and the highest unemployment in Northern Europe are the less famous of its problems, yet the most pressing. But still the myths prevail, insults from every quarter. Rabid Nationalist gunmen versus dour Presbyterian bigots: an unreasonable and bellicose bunch engaged in a 17th century religious war, fuelled by a cynical, ambivalent Republic and a mighty imperialist Britain. Whereas in reality, most of those involved are reasonable people with understandable fears and aspirations frozen in their responses to a situation which is out of anyone's control. The sheer hopelessness of the situation is the only hope. But the hope is there, and lives in the ordinary good sense of the people of the North. It is this good sense and humanity which is undermined by the insults of the world, the British and the Southern Irish. The insults take every form but find sustenance in the myths.

But *A Sense of Ireland* isn't happening just because the Irish are tired of the stereotypes, the Irish jokes and the accepted mythologies. It is more because the English are increasingly aware that these don't provide the truth which they are anxious to know. The trauma of Northern Ireland is also theirs.. Why *are* English boys dying on the streets of Belfast? What *is* this all about? What *is* Ireland? Who *are* the Irish? English people want answers that make sense, not catchwords and bogeys. All of the mystification of the past centuries must end if a way forward is to be found.

A Sense of Ireland is one small but significant contribution to that process. The name of this festival represents our aspiration that, by presenting a *sense* of what is happening today in the arts in Ireland, we may help to make some *sense* to our English neighbours of what we are as a people.

The changes in Ireland, outlined above, have created the climate for a startling upsurge of creative activity in all areas of the arts. These changes have also done much to destroy those vestiges of the past which gave credence to the myths, and to allow for a new self-confidence and self-image among the Irish, North and South. These two developments are closely linked, and it is desirable to be aware of both in order to appreciate either.

The destruction of the old barriers of censorship, sectarianism and underdevelopment which is in hand (albeit precariously) has found its clearest and healthiest expression in the media and the arts. Layered upon a strong and unique tradition of local cultural activity, we have experienced a blossoming of individual and collective creative concern. Film societies and production, galleries, camera clubs, craft centres and folk and rock venues, publishing houses, dance groups, and so on abound. The two Arts Councils and other bodies are branching out in all directions to cope with new interest and activity at community and metropolitan level. The commercial side is also thriving.

However, it must be stressed that while we are exuberant, we have few illusions. These changes are recent. They indicate a new awareness and confidence, and bode well for the future. But we are coming out of a long fallow period and much remains to be done. The circumstances that drove most of our creative resources abroad are only now in change. The situation in Ireland remains difficult and uncertain for the arts and the present 'renaissance' may prove to be a temporary release, rather than a new beginning. The final and most important reason for *A Sense of Ireland* lies in that dilemma.

As first conceived *A Sense of Ireland* was to have been a modest display of the avant-garde, mainly in one venue: a few conceptualists, some new independent film, an experimental theatre company. In retrospect I am glad that it went far beyond this, and pleased that I was encouraged by many to make it so. There are enough arbitrary divisions in Ireland and Britain already.

It was only worth doing if it said as much as possible, but more important if it exposed *everything* to sophisticated critical scrutiny. If the right lessons are learned, one sure guarantee that the present re-awakening in the arts in Ireland will avoid provincialism, complacency or recession is to take it outside and confront it with itself, unprotected. I have no doubts but that the knocks will be hard. We haven't gone through so many difficulties without being badly affected. But neither do I have doubts that both the durable and nascent qualities of the arts in Ireland will be recognised and will be helped by this entire and unprecedented experience, to develop further to fruition.

A Sense of Ireland spans the established and anti-establishment, the new and uncertain, the great tradition, the funny and the serious, the quiet and the loud. It makes no great claims nor any apologies. It is true and representative. It is there!

John Stephenson
Programme Director

SUNDAY AT THE ZOO.

Mr. Murphy. "EXCUSE ME, SORR; BUT CAN YE DIRECT ME TO THE GOIN' OUT INTRANCE?"

A British View of Ireland

I am, I suppose, as pure English as any Englishman — there has been talk of a Scots great-grandmother, but she died before I was born and left no particular fringe-celtic memories among her descendants. My first understanding of the Irish identity was the illustrations to a story in a fairy-tale book I had when I was maybe six. It was a narrative of a young fisher who took up in an unsatisfactory way with a stranded mermaid; and according to the pictures he lived in a very small turf-roofed cabin among stoney fields by the sea (Connemara?); he wore knee-breeches and a swallow-tail coat; his tapering top-hat had a clay pipe stuck in the band; he twirled a short shillelagh, and played on the flute. His mermaid, when she adopted human shape and married him, went about with bare feet and a shawl wrapped round her shoulders. At about the same time that I was impressed by this exotic couple, I began to be aware of an uncle who had married an Irish lady and lived as a school-master in Belfast. He was not often in England, and although when he did visit us he and his wife seemed much like anyone else, I could not remove from my mind the notion that their normal home sur-roundings and habiliments must be akin to those of western Connaught, circa 1800.

My only other contact with Ireland was a sort of extended family of immigrant labourers that lived in the next street to us in Barnsley. I fancy now that there would have been one couple who kept a lodging house for a number of unrelated and peripatetic young men. They were very unruly and the Yorkshire housewives of the more or less middle-class neighbourhood talked about them in scandalised whispers. They played football in the street, in shirt-sleeves, on Sundays; they played cards on the front doorsteps amid loud brawling; they were reputed not to have a clock in the house and to persecute nearby residences at unexpected intervals, begging for 'a sight of the time'

A few years later my Belfast uncle wrote to me saying that he had sent me a Christmas present of a book about Cuchulainn, a knowledge of whom he thought I should add to my enthusiasm for, Achilles, Odysseus, and King Arthur. The book never arrived and I was beast-ly disappointed. We wrote to him to tell him. He immediately sent another copy, explaining that the IRA had set off a bomb in the Belfast post office and probably my parcel had been a victim of the blast. I was told that IRA meant 'Irish Republican Army': I assumed this to be the army of Mr De Valera's 'free state' (they had taught us enough geography at school to account for Partition). I was puzzled because we had been at war with the Germans for some months, but, as far as I knew, the Irish were not involved. Yeats's evocation of Cuchulainn in

Water cresses, which they terme
shamrocks, rootes and other
herbes they feed vpon, otemeale
and butter they cramme
together, they drinke whey,
mylke, and biefe brothe. Fleshe
they devour without bread, and
that halfe raw; the rest boyleth in
their stomackes with Aqua Vitae,
which they swill in after such a
surfet by quartes & pottels; they
let their cowes bloud which,
growen to a gelly they bake and
overspred with butter, and so
late it in lumpes. No meat they
fansie so much as porke, and the
fater the better. One of John O
Neales household demaunded of
his fellow whether biefe were
better than porke; 'that', quoth
the other 'is as intricate a
question, as to aske whether
thou art better than Oneale'.

from The disposition and maners
of the meere Irish, commonly
called the wyld Irish.
'Holinshed's Irish Chronicle'
(1577)

18

direct juxtaposition with events at another post office was not to become familiar to me for a good many years.

During the war, when Ireland's neutrality, so witlessly misrepresented by the English and to the English, permeated almost every reference to that country that one could meet, I learnt my English history in greater depth and discovered that at nearly every stage in the tale the Irish were *being a nuisance*. We read how Cromwell had made the streets of Drogheda and Wexford 'run with blood' — the first time I had come across this figure of speech, which was thus all the more vivid and disgusting, and quite upset the generally favourable view of the Protector taken by the textbook. If our guarantor of English liberty had also been a murderous ogre, what could not such contradictions do for Churchill — or, vice versa, Hitler — in days to come? One's childish certainties were horribly disturbed. At that time, remember, there were air-raids, a real threat of Nazi invasion, fathers of school-fellows reported dead in action — we needed so badly to be reassured that our country was always right, and was always bound to win because the other side was always wrong . . .

I came for a period to resent the Irish very strongly. But subterraneously, so to speak, because I had such small experience of them. My uncle in Belfast was a Protestant, as — so I believed — was the entire population of the Six Counties: I knew he had gone to pains to learn Irish and that he spent his holidays in the Ulster Gaeltacht: I had no idea that his colleagues and neighbours in the Malone Road might think this rather an undesirable thing to do (in fact I have been told the RUC Special Branch were following him all over town — they thought he must be at least pro-German, if not an actual Abwehr agent): and I had also no idea that the border between the good Irish and the troublesome ones afforded all sorts of people far removed from the IRA cause for a much more mature resentment than my own juvenile splutterings. I read in the *Meccano Magazine* that the Irish railways had just built a brand new express locomotive called 'Macha' — how dare De Valera refuse to fight Hitler and yet grace his public transport with so splendid and legendary a name? Cuchulainn and the goddess of Emain were after all as much my property as his — had my uncle not sent me the book? Were not the stories all set in *Ulster*?

I have gone into some detail about these early prejudices because they seem to me typical of what like to be thought the Educated Classes of Britain. If I had not found myself in later years, more or less accidentally, mixing, marrying and working with Irish people, and in Ireland itself, I have no doubt that the same attitudes (glazed with a degree of adult

Robert Ballagh. 'Inside No. 3'

sophistication, to be sure) would have remained firmly with me well into the 1970s. They have certainly been at the back of much of the British politicians' and news-persons' pronouncements that have recently become so tediously familiar: and they have done no good to anyone in any part of either country.

Oh dear, here I am about to diverge from the personal into something that smacks of politics. Is it possible though to talk about an Englishman's view of Ireland these days without bringing in the horrid subject? I could state, for example, that as a cradle-Protestant I have lived for the past decade amongst allegedly priest-ridden cradle-Catholics without the least feeling that I was any more of an outsider (or 'blow-in') than, say, a Catholic Dubliner might have felt in the same Co Galway village. But such a declaration would inevitably ring a resonance north of the border, and my use of the word 'blow-in' might be thought by some unfortunate, as it has been used in an Irish election to vilify civil-liberties activists . . . I could ramble agreeably about west of Ireland folk customs and survivals: but then I might easily slip into reminiscence of how the other Christmas three local teenagers came 'mumming' to my cottage door after dark and nearly made me pass out with uncontrollable fear because their festive getup (based on balaclavas with eyeholes, and peaked caps) was the exact fac-simile of the disguises assumed by what the press calls 'motiveless murderers' in the North. . . . I could offer anecdotes of the striking 'characters' to be encountered in Galway and Iar-Connacht — the lawyer, the film-maker, the freelance journalist — but so many of such people are on someone's list of 'political unreliables', and in a catalogue for a non-sectarian arts festival one could only describe the Book-of-Kells intricacies of their conversations by in-serting self-censoring finger-to-nosebridge gaps, like a policeman reporting swear-words in court . . . I could even do you some gossip in the Somerville/Ross style about the quirks of the Garda Siochana: but then I might find myself mentioning how they came to my residence to look for kidnapped Dr Herrema — I can't imagine why they thought I should have him, and I have certainly no idea why, when they found he was not in the living-room, they didn't think to look in the loft, or even in the bed-rooms, but . . . you see what I mean? You might also perhaps see that the sort of society I am talking about might have been made for a playwright to live in and to draw inspiration from.

Arts festivals of course are not about any of this, as a rule. They are congenial oppor-tunities for the selected invitees to congratulate themselves upon their adherence to the noblest generalisations — harmony, shared humanity, abhorrence of violence and what not (always with a tacit reservation in favour of at least one dubious habit of whoever happens to be generalising at the time. My law-'n-order is your brutal terrorism and contrariwise).

It can be a good idea to hang a decorative curtain over an alcove full of old bones: but not if people are allowed to mistake it for a solid wall. And were not the original whited sepulchres denounced in the Gospel as the product of a community environmental initiative supported by all right-thinking Jerusalem opinion? If the 'arts' cannot recognise and elucidate and honestly present inherent conflicts of principle and national and social interest, then we might as well just pack it in. I do hope this festival will be able to find for itself that sort of back bone. Irish arts are not British. If on occasion they appear to the British public rebarbative and inimical, they will only be being true to themselves. If everything is to be enjoyed and assimilated in London like a cup of Complan, then something will have gone wrong. A nation in which 'wiser counsels' have prevailed is a mendacious nation: I do not believe that Ireland is that yet, despite its frequent self-reproaches of hypocrisy, moral cowardice, inferiority complex. . . All very allusive and enigmatical, I know. Let me conclude with an allusive quote from the story of Cuchulainn.

' "Let all the poets and the womenfolk go to Cuchulainn", said the king, "and take him to the Valley of the Deaf; and make carousal and amusements and skilful entertainments, so that he shall not hear the incitements of the hosts trying to perplex him". . . "Alas", said Cuchulainn, "Great are these cries that I hear as they plunder the entire province; and for that, the end of my victorious career has come, and the province has reached the brink of doom." "Let that pass, it is nothing but a false and evanescent host of winds and there is nothing in it but deception." And they began to drink and entertain themselves for another while until they all heard the great cries outside. . . Those who were guarding Cuchulainn themselves set up cries and arguments and sports around him – but Cuchulainn did not believe anything they said: and he ordered Laegh to catch the horses and prepare the chariot. . .'

Bear in mind that this story is by no means simplistic. They were guarding Cuchulainn from what they believed with good reason were phantoms: and yet behind the phantoms were genuine physical enemies: the hero eventually met death at their hands. His friends had proved even more deluded than he was: and the Valley of the Deaf had been no fit place for any of them.

John Arden

England on a Clear Day

An Irish view of the English

We know more about the English than they know about us. This is partly because the conquered one, the servant, the retainer, nearly always does know more about his lord and master than that superior and largely indifferent being knows about him. It is also because the Irish, like the other peoples on the Celtic fringe, the Welsh and the Scots, are on the whole better educated, class for class and person for person, than the English are. They have the same passion for education in general; and they have, as all the world knows, a particular passion for history. Probably the have-nots always think more about history than the haves; it is, after all, in the interests of possessing classes and peoples to forget about history, which is largely a record of how possessions were acquired; and consequently they are inclined to pretend that it did not happen, or that it was about ideas and noble abstractions and not about conquest and seizure and dispossession.

Anyway the Irish do think and care a lot about history. Even our daily newspapers are, somewhat to the amazement of visitors, full of discussions of historical cause and effect; political parties are rooted in particular and often conflicting interpretations of historical crises and developments; and though the debate about history has never ceased in the present writer's lifetime at least, it has of course taken on a new acerbity and a new complexity since the eruption of – to use the easy locution – 'the Northern troubles'.

But it is impossible to know anything at all about Irish history without also knowing a great deal about English: about Henry VIII and the English Reformation, about Elizabeth and the Spanish threat, about Cromwell and Pitt and Gladstone. An Englishman could pass for someone who knew a bit about his country's history while having only a very hazy idea about Charles Stewart Parnell. An Irishman who knew nothing about William Ewart Gladstone would be an ignoramus.

And although quite large numbers of Englishmen feel a general sort of diffused sympathy for Ireland, some, as we know too well, have been smitten by what they consider to be the charm of the people or the country, and a few, like the first Erskine Childers, have become unassuageable supporters of the Irish cause, not many have been impressed by what could be called the sum total of the Irish achievement in the way that large numbers of Irish men and women have been impressed by what they regard as the sum total of the English achievement.

Those English who have expressed admiration for Ireland in fairly recent times have been mostly of a literary bent, and what has impressed them has been what seemed a remarkable

Richard Haughton

abundance of talent and high spirits, often brought to bear on English life or subjects, as by Sheridan, Shaw and Wilde. Even where our literature in English is concerned, though, few Englishmen have succeeded in identifying the comic Irish vision with its elements of human camaraderies as clearly as many Irishmen have succeeded in identifying the calm English vision with its elements of human hope. In expressing praise of Shakespeare, Wordsworth, Blake, Dickens and D.H. Lawrence, it seems natural to praise England and the English people; less natural in the case of Joyce or Beckett to praise Ireland and the Irish people.

Nor, leaving Irish literature in English aside, have other specifically Irish things – the fierce continuity of the Gaelic tradition, the proclaimed egalitarianism of the Republican, for example – seemed as remarkable or as admirable to such proportionately large numbers of English people as certain specifically English things – the stability of institutions, the genius for compromise, the assumption of equality before the law, for instance – have seemed to large numbers of Irish people. And, apart from the fact that we know more about them than they do about us, and that there may even be more to admire – for England after all has had a history, and we have not – the reasons are not really very far to seek. From the language to the legal system many things English have been successfully transplanted to Ireland. From the form of parliamentary assembly with its two major parties downwards, many English models are working and can be seen to be working more or less successfully in the new environment. Some of these transplants were accomplished by force, others of them by

Richard Haughton

fraud: no matter, accomplished they were; and to such an extent that a very real if largely subconscious and unexpressed feeling exists among very many people in Ireland that without the English connection Ireland would still be a somewhat backward and benighted place.

The common and simplistic view on the other side of the channel is, I know, that the Irish are natively and stubbornly 'anti-English'. That a sort of anti-English feeling, some of it quite rationally and logically grounded in fact, exists, no-one would deny, although it waxes and wanes very much according to the circumstances of the moment; but it is also true that a much larger number of Irish people than are usually credited with it or would ever wish to articulate it, have, somewhere at the backs of their minds, the idea that England is the source and the English connection the safeguard of civilisation in this island.

This attitude, it is important to stress, differs from the many that used to be defined by the Irish word *shoneenism*, the attitudes that made obeisance to Dublin Castle and the pathetic values of the vice-regal court. It is, for one thing, less obviously connected with greed, personal advantage or mere snobbism; indeed where certain forms of promotion and personal advantage are concerned those who hold it may deem it somewhat politic to suppress it or conceal it. But the fact remains that many, many people in southern Ireland feel, consciously or otherwise (the feeling takes of course much more obvious, cruder and more identifiable forms in the north) that without England there would be no habeas corpus and trial by jury, no safeguards for personal freedom and scarcely any law and order; that beyond the English connection all is jobbery, obscurantism, envy, narrow-mindedness and the love of rapine and slaughter for their own sakes.

And just as anti-English feeling has its rational and its rational-historical side, so has this sort of pro-English sentiment. Urban civilisation and certain developed forms of trade and commerce, manufactury and exploitation in Ireland were for many centuries dependent on keeping the native Irishry beyond a pale which had an actual physical existence. The native Irish legal system did not run to habeas corpus and trial by jury. Neither, it might be added, did it run to gaols, transportation, massive confiscations of territory and the naked exploitation of resources by private individuals for their own gain; but no matter. The circumstances of Irish history and the limited forms of pacification achieved in England's interest by English law, always gave a colour to the belief that the appeal to violence came from the Irish side. They still do; and, the conflict in the north-eastern corner of the island aside for the moment, even the cruel events of the civil war of 1922-23, the English-inspired quarrel over an English-dictated document, at once made it seem as if all the gloomy prognostications that had been made throughout the period of Home Rule agitation about the bloodshed that would follow loosening of the English connection were amply justified.

Now much of this feeling has been handed down as a sort of heritage from one possessing class in Ireland to another: from the Cromwellian settler to the eighteenth century trader or manufacturer, from the landowner to the Catholic merchant who came into his own after the passing of the Emancipation Act; but it also has an identifiable connection with trades and avocations. Lawyers, after all, like the law. Parliamentarians like parliament. And though there are of course nationalist judges and lawyers, and very few of our southern parliamentarians would get elected if they did not make some sort of obeisance to old nationalist gods and shibboleths, on the whole lawyers tend to be firm admirers of English legal precedents, while the tendency of our legislature and our legal draughtsmen to cling as closely as possible to existent English models, new or old, is notorious.

Which brings us to poets and literary men in general, who write the language of Shakespeare, John Dryden and Samuel Johnson: write it of course with varying degrees of sensitivity, awareness and knowledge of the English tradition, but write it all the same. If you believe with Theobald Matthew Wolfe Tone (as the present writer does) that 'the connection between Ireland and England is the curse of the Irish nation' and, as a matter of intellectual if not emotional conviction therefore that 'our independence must be had at all hazards'; and if you yet rejoice in using the English language and inheriting your share of its glories, you are, at first blush anyway, in a somewhat ambiguous position. To the outside observer it would appear at first as if you ought to belong to that portion of the Irish people who believe that the English connection is really, in one way or another, the source of all sweetness and all light and therefore must be, in one way or another, at all costs preserved.

In the days of my own mis-spent youth the question of being an Irish poet who used the English language as distinct from being an English one who did the same used to be the subject of endless, fruitless and really very woolly minded, not to say dishonest, debate; and I got a shock recently when I opened an issue of the English magazine *Aquarius* to find that such a debate was still dragging its weary and disconsolate length along. The fact is, though, that it was a Scottish issue; and the pages had been thrown open to the Scots to thrash around in on the subject of 'What it feels like to be a Scottish poet'. I read it with amazement and a feeling of *déjà vu* and horror for the days of yore so strong as to be stifling (forbye there were some intelligent contributions). But when I asked myself why these fusty old debates were no longer conducted hereabouts, the only answer I could find was the degree of independence we have achieved as compared to the Scots.

This is partly a political, or, more specifically, an institutional matter. We have an apparatus of discussion, criticism and propagation which they do not have, an apparatus which, like all such nowadays, is partly dependent on the state. We have an amount of publishing which would have been inconceivable a few years ago. But it is also partly a matter of confidence. The enormous and more or less simultaneous acquisition of Joyce and Yeats as founding fathers of a modern literature means that we have a tradition of our own to work in. It would be wrong to say that this frees us from Matthew Arnold, Thomas Hardy and W.H. Auden, nor would it be a good thing if it did; for to a writer using the English language the presence in his consciousness (or his unconsciousness, if you prefer it that way) of the great masters of the English tongue is an important matter which he would be the poorer without.

What it does mean is that we can take them or leave them in a way which was once not possible, any more than it was possible for the American poets who preceded Whitman, poets like Longfellow, Whittier or even Edgar Allan Poe to take or leave their English models or forbears. It is true that almost from the beginning of Irish literature in English there was an

attempt to establish a sort of independence both in idiom and subject. This led to the excesses of un-natural Hiberno-English known as "Kiltartan" as well as to a restriction of subject matter in favour of the primitive, the tradition-bound, the patriarchal and the archaic. In other words the writers concerned were Irish with malice aforethought, literary nationalists with a national and not just a human stock-in-trade. And from the time of the so-called Irish Revival, the Celtic twilight period on, there was an evident paradox in the situation: the English, starved of pastoral as their countryside disappeared, starved of the mythological, starved of the primitive in their mock-Tudor suburbs, responded with glee. Both parties were, in their way, happy.

Well, all that is now coming to an end I am glad to say. Though there are still lingering traces of the mentality which created it, the Irish Revival, with its implications of a literature-less past just escaped and an esoteric hinterland which had an appeal because of its mere strangeness, is, thankfully, almost over. The Celtic twilight, or fog, is being dispersed. We are very nearly free from the picturesque, the romantic-rural, the nostalgic-archaic, the historical-archaeological, the tribal subconscious as our only modes. And the truth is that we are free from these deliberately nationalist, and therefore, in a deep sense truly provincial modes which appealed even to the early Yeats and to the later and less spontaneous O'Casey, precisely because we have won for ourselves a greater degree of national independence and national self-confidence in the matter of literature. (There are those who don't know that yet, but no matter.)

And hopefully too that blissful state will sooner or later apply in politics. I have dwelt at greater length on what I believe to be a curious current of pro-English feeling in this country than I have on the much-better publicised degree of anti-English sentiment, though on the subject of the latter, one should be wary of confusing a practical desire to end a political connection with anything that could be called anti-English feeling. However, pro or anti feelings are both undesirable. They feed on each other and they hinder all sort of natural development. There is good reason to look forward to the day when, free from either, we can at length come to terms with all things English if only because, with its advent, many Irish people will also be able to see things Irish in a clearer light.

Anthony Cronin

In London with the Cargo Cult

An Irish Experience in Britain

If there are more wreaths than lovers laid in Ireland, then in Britain I discovered there's more dreams than concrete laid to rest. My first experience of Britain was of a modest civil-engineering nature, using a JCB1 — a shovel — to dig holes and spread concrete. Now, a decade later, those bouts of labour ended, I'm constantly surprised on passing certain tower blocks to note that they haven't collapsed. I have been greatly transformed by the decade and I wonder whether similar inner processes haven't been at work on them.

Equally, I've benefited enormously from living in this domesticated nation of oblique brokers. The seductive quality of British apathy is probably the final acid test and hallmark of total integration. It seems to me a cultivated antidote and refreshing counterbalance to the morbid fatalism of Ireland — usually kept at bay by hysterical monologues and with laughter without the possibility of exchange. Generally it seems that the deluge of raw and unrefined feelings unleashed by Ireland and visited on her bemused children, finds no home here, turns inward, sour and subversive of the individual. Or else, becomes the howling mewling roaring madness of the professional Irish abroad. Nobody can step out of history, but the pain of coming to terms with it can be immense. So the apathy doesn't come easily and must be nurtured. Between bawling songs and having a slither on the boards, it finally dawns that 'Them' is 'Us' and that the Irish, like every minority group in Britain, have something important to live out. But with the eighth consecutive century of the same tragi-comedy, it's clear that changes are imminent in the casting and production.

In addition, one of the most vital experiences associated with living in London over the last decade has been to witness the delivery of parcels from the past. Daemonic dancers, sufi musicians and the whole gamut of Third World drama have all been here but very little has actually touched the hairy underbelly of John Bull. All of these productions are the most visible and acceptable expression of some or other minority group, otherwise isolated and taciturn in the outward calm of Britain. It's all unfinished business coming home to rest or cause dismay, depending on how the parcel is packaged. Day and night, vessels dock bearing cargoes of the imagination, of cries that weren't heard or of things that weren't said; much of it the detritus of an imperial past, transformed and returned. Having quite pragmatically deemed the empire finished, there is understandable alarm each time a vessel is sighted and its cargo, duly pronounced of British origin, is brought into the light. With all of this debris lying about, more than ample for endless drama, British audiences may forget how much else is being returned with each production, poem or novel. I can recall one evening sitting in the Old Vic when the laughs were few for 'The Playboy' simply because the street theatre of Ulster had obtruded most savagely that very day. Or the morning following Bloody Sunday when I was verbally mugged by otherwise apathetic and pleasant colleagues in the newspaper where I worked.

At the same time, the 'ould' pragmatism does not work any longer, the new calendar of stagflation reigns supreme. Like the currency, authority has been devalued and grossly inflated and nibbled away at by every minority, both homegrown and foreign, a process to which the Irish have contributed their pagan mite. So that the only reliable means of seeing Britain becomes akin to that of the British themselves, perceived and judged through institutions of decreasing affinity or relevance to the individual. And new institutions arise which everyone can join, as with the club of one and a half million unemployed, 'spalpeens' all, to jockey for position in a new alignment of traditions. While everyone might agree that authority has suffered the death of a thousand cuts, veritable armadas loaded with the inner debris of the past wait to offload and return what had long ago been taken to the farthest corners of the world.

Synchronistically, the BBC translates other versions of that past into drama series of ravishing beauty. The media becomes a gigantic reconditioning industry, increasingly offensive as it becomes more popular in assuring a continuity in the face of rapid and alarming transformation. Never having anyhow invested much belief in that continuity, like most Irish I both enjoy and deplore this great national pastime, a mirror-image of what had been left behind in Ireland. Thus, with cargoes from the past arriving by the hour, immigrants are on hand as stevedores of the imagination or as menacing desperadoes of the spirit, wildly keen to interpret what has been returned and to entice Britain to take back what she left behind. For the Irish it's a learning process, whether they like it or not, to breathe life into the spirit of things before those images are reconditioned beyond recognition, emasculated and co-opted into a hierarchy of tradition. More popularly, it's a cargo cult in reverse.

In confusing circumstances of a routed economy, my own experience has been of the immense and growing rift in Britain between what is offered by the imagination and what is actually lived. The baffled citizens are thus left without a bridge, aside from television images resembling animated postage stamps. To liberate the images from that tiny screen, it's important that vast numbers of foreigners should always live in Britain. Or, at least living in London whence they can occasionally venture on expeditions into the stillness of England.

The Abbey Theatre: 'Waiting for Godot'

For at the appropriate moment they can lean forward and without raising their voices, nod amiably, identifying various bits of flotsam from the past. The Irish role in that reclamation is important at present for the final ebb tide is now concentrated again in Ireland, where it began and where, unavoidably, it must end.

Not that there is anything especially difficult about identification — though there is a marked reluctance to take back what is theirs. And I no longer know whether to cry or laugh when my hosts politely indicate that Ireland is 'boring', such innocence impresses and deflates me considerably. While it's true that other civilisations never went wild on rabbits or domestic pets as transcendental symbols, Britain has managed to elevate them to that level. It is a secret language designed to confound the foreigner, a surrealist language which must be mastered before any exchange commences. I waver in my devotion to this task, continually inclined to drag up monster hounds and sea-cats instead of the versions more acceptable to the British psyche. Hence, I've encountered a stubborn resistance when trying to link Irish symbols to British ways. Like the Shavian sugared pill, the important symbols lie largely ignored on another borderline, just above the low tide mark, on Crown territory.

I've contributed to the cargo cult in my own way. Arriving ten years ago to live in central London and inside my jacket, sewn almost into my skin was a rogues' gallery of alien faces. These faces ranged across the entire span of years shared by Britain and Ireland. Each one was emblematic of something which I had been bequeathed from the past, whether Elizabethan or Fenian, spectral or concrete. Over the years, by sly encounters and angry exchanges, I managed to match the rogues to living faces and thus returned gifts I hadn't sought nor which had stood me in good stead. Having done that however, I was surprised to discover more faces emerging through that lining, replenishing the spots left vacant. Finally and with initial reluctance, I had to concede honour and position to my very own rogues' gallery. And that has been what Britain has given me, the experience has been of time and opportunity to trade beneficially in a past both personal and more diffuse.

Through Pythonesque exchanges with forlorn British exiles in their own land, I have found a way of scanning that experience. And as irony seems just about the only worthwhile element in common between the Irish and the British — aside from violence though infinitely more enjoyable, the trek across the inner British landscape has been a journey of discovery and enjoyment. Perhaps the journey could have taken place anywhere under the sun but it was certainly given fresh impetus and awful immediacy by the war in Ulster whose meaning had to be shared.

I have also come to accept that as the greatest exponents of partition in recent history, the British have naturally partitioned themselves into little bits and pieces. Beneath the patina of politeness which is invaluable as it allows people who detest one another to spend time together, chaos and total irrationality bubble away. This has reached a level of such potency that they no longer know how to reassemble their own jigsaw, since they obdurately refuse to recognise particular pieces as belonging to the puzzle. So the cycle of seasons continues, from winter depression to summer inflation, with the odd currency crisis thrown in for light relief, from a society wanting the mothering of socialism to the strident piratical machismo of the Tories. And with that inevitability, the only way of seeing how the bits may eventually fit together, for me at least, has been through works of the imagination Britain inspires, the sluice-gates of the unconscious, where the borders are breached and hot-pursuit applies.

I was initially daunted by all of those borders and boundaries, but have come to realise that I can pick and choose whichever ones I care to observe and that is a change from Ireland where borders of any kind have historically and personally engendered neither comprehension nor respect. So that by living in London, I have a more sanguine sense of Ireland just as, by traipsing through Asia for a British newspaper I learned much about how to view Britain. In both cases, the experiences have been transferred, quite successfully, back to London. One of the most interesting lessons regarding Britain arose from an evening spent in Calcutta. There, in recounting an anecdote about a south Indian city of about half a million people, a husband was interrupted by his wife who helpfully put the story in context by mentioning — 'remember, we were the only people there'. I fell from my chair laughing but everyone else found the comment quite in order. Well, that still happens quite a bit and each time it constellates a whole new vision of Britain for me. The cargoes keep on arriving and I confess to being one of the wreckers who helpfully waves a storm lantern to get the stuff onshore as soon as possible.

Rory Flanagan

The Artist in Ireland

In that unfortunately famous fifth section of *Under Ben Bulben*, Yeats advises Irish poets to 'Scorn the sort now growing up'. The low-born deformities to which he goes on to refer probably constitute a fair percentage of the older generation of this island and they have indeed had their share of scorn. Since the Censorship Act of 1929 the Irish artist has been encouraged to believe that the hostility of Society (especially of the middle-class and Catholic or of the working class and Catholic-Gaelic or of the Protestant and bitter type) is necessary for the True Artist. A certain amount of what Beckett has called *rigor vitae* has been easily found among Irish artists for over forty years.

But since the mid-sixties Ireland has changed so much that most of the conventions which once dictated the relationship between artist and society have vanished, save from the minds of those still consoled by what once was true. Ireland performed the remarkable feat of becoming a consumer society without having the natural resources or the industrial base which normally support such a system. The intricate game of financial and commercial monopoly which has been proceeding over the last twenty years has created a climate in which art has itself become one of the commodities in which people deal. Reputations, first editions, paintings and sculpture, commissioned music, commissioned theatre are now all an integral part of the cultural scene. Arts Council subsidies and tax-free artists, an increasing academic industry in the history and tradition of Irish art have all combined to dispel the notion that exile is any longer a necessity. A climate of liberal opinion has created an undiscriminating respect for the artist and his products.

As a consequence, the position of the artist has become more difficult than it once was. Within certain and rather strict limits, Society is willing to offer welcome and compromise. The idea of alienation has almost entirely lost its heroic or subversive aspect. Instead, it has become popularised. The artist wears his isolation as the businessman wears his suit, regularly and expectedly. In fact, the artist is no longer tied to some notion of relationship between himself and Society. The State has replaced Society and nothing has yet come along to entirely replace the fetish of isolation. At least that was the case up to 1968 when the North finally began its long and reluctant collapse. The effect was at first tonic. Violence, publicity, the Irish question all came alive together. The famished fifties disappeared; the revolutionary sixties seemed to supply an endless stream of material for paintings, novels, plays and poems. These inevitably came; a number of them also went; but the North stayed grimly on, unsolved and apparently insoluble. Since there was no substantial tradition of dissent in Ireland, only a tendency towards dissension, the artists found themselves awash in an historical crisis and, simultaneously, falsely consoled by the liberal consumerism which was willing to greet any artistic rendering of the crises which would not involve any political commitment to or demand for its resolution. Some artists have felt obliged to attempt to deal with the general crisis; some have felt equally to ignore it. The general public has responded well to any attempt to aestheticise contemporary politics and sullenly to attempt to politicise art. Such is the nature of consumerism.

Other forces are also at work, some of them so enduring that they seem almost inevitable parts of the Irish condition. In 1930, Shaw felt obliged to defend his departure from Dublin on the grounds that a professional man or an artist 'must have a metropolitan domicile and an international culture: that is, he felt that his first business was to get out of Ireland'. Many before and many since have felt the same way, although, of course, this whole attitude is heresy against the true Church of the Irish Revival which made such a virtue of staying-at-home, close-to-the-soil. Indeed, October 1979 has witnessed an English poet say that 'In England we either envy or despise the Irish as peasants.' That's an antiquated attitude which would have warmed many Irish literary bosoms some fifty years ago. But there is indeed an element of absurdity in the Irish claim to a specific literary tradition (to take the most obvious example) when there is only a small and burgeoning Irish publishing industry. It is certainly possible to be published in Ireland; but to have work distributed abroad by an Irish publisher is another matter entirely. The size of the Irish public is insufficient to support a large-scale industry. Therefore the question does constantly arise – can such an island ever be anything other than peripheral to the metropolitan centres? Can it ever escape the risk of provincialism, one perhaps intensified by its long colonial history? Can it ever achieve a harmonious relationship with the English culture to which it is so politically hostile? Dublin's claim to centrality for Irish culture is always at risk because of London's claim to be the capital or one of the capitals of the English speaking world.

Naturally, to mention the language is to raise another issue. In Ireland there is a culture far older than the English speaking one. It is also, in many respects, far weaker. In music and in literature, to some extent in painting and sculpture, it exercises an imaginative influence upon Irish artists which is far greater than any influence it can bring to bear politically or commercially. This resource, fast-fading as it may be, is often regarded as that which finally distinguishes Ireland from all other nations. The Holy Grail of Irishness can be pursued here with some hope of being found. Yet it is obvious that the economic forces which dictate the island's development will either destroy that culture or make it even more vestigial than it now is. Not for the first time, Ireland reveals itself to be in the paradoxical position of doing away with the very thing on which it lays its claim to identity and difference. Again the artist finds himself in a curiously ambivalent position here. The degree to which the country becomes metropolitan (and not provincial) is determined by its success in ceasing to be Gaelic. There are other ways of posing this problem but to put it in these brutal terms is to highlight the nature of a problem which is both a political and an artistic one.

The congruence between political and artistic problems in Ireland has been often dramatic and always potentially lethal for the artist. A culture still suffering from an inflamed self-consciousness tends to make strident demands of its artists. In this century in particular Ireland has often sought in its art an image of itself which would, in some heroic or memorable way, compensate for the obvious failure of national politics. Artists have refused or succumbed to the stress; a few, like AE or Yeats have taken it and their work has gained in confidence and muscularity from the struggle. But in addition, the artist has generally felt himself to be more exposed than is usual to the slings and arrows of Irish misfortune because there has not been any protection afforded to him by any group, freelance or corporately employed, which could be called an intelligentsia. There must be few ex-colonies in the world in which an Intelligentsia has not flourished. Ireland is one of them. The universities have provided little or nothing in this area; the Church has not been an encouraging influence either. Thus the artist finds himself in a constellation all his own. The inhibiting reputation of the Irish as practitioners of what Virginia Woolf once called 'the soft cadence', that capacity for uproarious eloquence or crepuscular blather, has been a sad inheritance for most Irish authors. On top of that, other kinds of Irish artists have justifiably felt that their situation was more desperately limited still, since writing seemed to be the only recognised form of Irish art for so long a time. The reasons for these clichés, their emergence and their distressing endurance, have never been fully investigated. It seems unlikely that the artists, as a group, can investigate it in any comprehensive way. That is the task of an intelligentsia. Perhaps the failure of the Irish revolution earlier in this century and the hostility to any form of radicalism in politics evinced by the new and narrowminded State has postponed the emergence of any articulate intellectual constituency. Whatever the reason, the effect on Irish artists has not been good. They have been compelled to find a rationale for their art, they have been forced to engage in a frontal way with political crisis to such an extent that the practice of art has itself become problematic and even, on occasion, impossible. The lack of political stability and confidence on this island may energise art in some respect. But the failure to understand that failure is just as frequently damaging.

This festival, then, is more than a presentation of Irish art and artists to an English or to a London audience. In a sense, it is a presentation of Ireland to itself. We will perhaps be the better able to see ourselves because the presentation takes place on a foreign stage. And yet what foreignness could be more intimate than that between England and Ireland, Dublin and London. In some respects, although the range of artistic endeavour is wide, it will be clear that some arts are still emergent and in sore need of support while others, more established, or more popular, run the risk of confusing support with success. Film, dance, music, theatre, painting, photography are all expensive arts to practice and to produce on a scale like this. It would obviously be ungracious to criticise the fact that they are supported with the generosity displayed here. Equally it would be foolish to ignore the consequences for art and for its audience of the existence of this kind of support. There is, in the very existence of this festival, a clear declaration that one kind of relationship between art and society has almost ceased to be. Art can only be disloyal to itself; in supporting it we attempt now to persuade it to be loyal to whatever form of truth it can embody. In doing so we sponsor and present not only a sense of Ireland but, with that, a sense of truth, not limited to Ireland but emerging from its unique circumstances and from its stressful condition.

Seamus Deane

. . .To an Irishman who has
any sort of social conscience,
the conception of Ireland as a
romantic picture, in which the
background is formed by the
lakes of Killarney by moonlight,
and a round tower or so, whilst
every male figure is 'a broth of a
bhoy' and every female one is a
colleen in a crimson Connemara
cloak, is as exasperating as the
conception of Italy as a huge
garden and art museum in-
habited by picturesque artists'
models, is to a sensible Italian.

G B Shaw 1.2.1896

Oisin Kelly: Tern '74

Art Exhibitions

'Clara and Dario' An installation by Seamus Coleman in Milan

Two slide projectors project images in continuation. The projections are twin-synchronized and programmed by a continuous tape on which the audio is also recorded.

Any two images are in relationship with each other and with the audio. Interpretation of the images is related to the sequence of both projections and the audio, the images/audio are the events (narrative). The visual narrative becomes a 'continuous' with the audio. Interpretation of the events develop from:
the order of the images of each projection with the audio; cross-correlation of the simultaneous projections with the audio.

Repetition and duration of the dialogue and projections provoke changing psychological associations and 'cause-effect' relationships of the events.

James Coleman Artist

Nigel Rolfe

Michael O'Sullivan

Many forms of modern art are devoid of rules. The artist makes his own. However formless or chaotic the manifestation, it is art if it expresses something, possibly something bad and negative.

Even our own pathetic and untidy advance guards, who have never learnt to draw, are artists because they express artistically (and convincingly) the fact that they can't draw.

Flann O Brien

'Running': A recent Nigel Rolfe installation/performance in Belfast

'– Whhoorish! shouted a sergeant; is it treadin' on th' tile of me coat yez want to be now? Oirish, an' prawd of it, wot?'

'– Ay, and so as to again excel in carving rich and diversified designs on all churches, within and without the walls; to build round towers higher than the high ones already here; to have multitudes of great bells and lesser bells aloft in bunches in all suitable and desirable places; and to have piles of rare images, altars, gems, and hundreds of square miles of painted glass for all our church windows.'

'– And mike Iahland a plice fit for 'eroes to live in, Paddy, eh wot?'

Sean O'Casey

Cecil King

'An Intrusion'. A recent work by Martin Gale

1. Deborah Brown   2. Charlie Tyrrell

— I pinched it out of the skivvy's room, Buck Mulligan said. It does her all right. The aunt always keeps plainlooking servants for Malachi. Lead him not into temptation. And her name is Ursula.

Laughing again, he brought the mirror away from Stephen's peering eyes.
— The rage of Caliban at not seeing his face in a mirror, he said. If Wilde were only alive to see you.

Drawing back and pointing, Stephen said with bitterness:
— It is a symbol of Irish art. The cracked lookingglass of a servant.

James Joyce
from 'Ulysses'

Brian King

Robert Ballagh

'I never had any access to the culture that many people think is *the* Irish culture, the rural Gaelic tradition. I can't paint Connemara fishermen. I never heard of folksong in my childhood or traditional music; they weren't played on the radio then.

My experience of Ireland is an urban Dublin one and I paint that. It would be dishonest of me to paint anything else. But being Dublin is being Irish.'

Robert Ballagh Artist

'I've withdrawn from the international stream of art to a more human and personal style than before. I found in my big abstract works that I couldn't say things that I felt like saying. I had arrived at a totally aesthetic art with no literary connotations. I wanted to make statements, using sarcasm or pun, and wit, and all of these I couldn't do. . . '

'You have to go back into what you are, to your culture and your nationality, the whole muddle of sentiment and politics, with myself in the middle.'
Miss O'Murphy? 'She is my Mother Ireland. Why? Because she was a whore!'

Micheal Farrell Artist

Michael Farrell

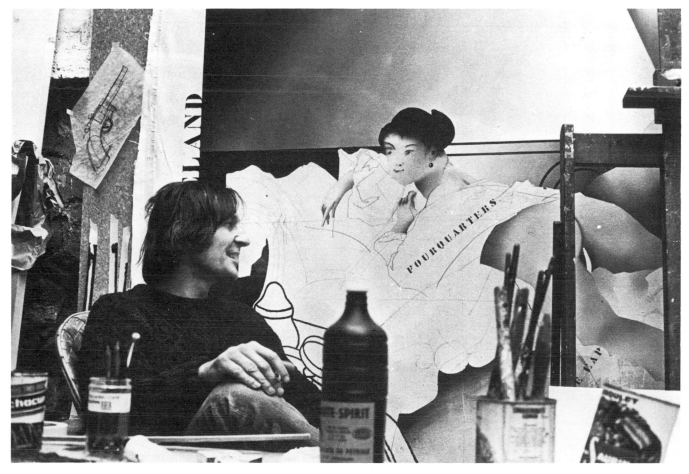

Erik Adriann Van der Grijn

'It's evident that Ireland has been a source of stimulation with its ingenuous adaptions of traffic signs, hazards, railings to the background landscapes, a combination which I respect in its uniqueness and which has intrigued me for years. The ''yellow'' fascination, dangerous and yet an obvious point of recognition, actually derived from childhood but on arrival in Ireland in 1964 I saw the yellow/black publicly manufactured against a background of ''wet'' greens and transient skies.''

Erik van der Grijn

'Florencecourt 1': TP Flanagan

We have no prairies
To slice a big sun at evening —
Everywhere the eye concedes to
Encroaching horizon,

Is wooed into the cyclops' eye
Of a tarn. Our unfenced country
Is bog that keeps crusting
Between the sights of the sun.

Seamus Heaney
from 'Bogland', for T P Flanagan

'Tree, Knockalough': Brian Bourke

Art is the human disposition
of sensible or intelligible
matter for an aesthetic end

James Joyce

The use of rational process in the making of art gives a specific character to the work which differentiates it from other more subjective attitudes. These differences make themselves apparent at both the visual and conceptual levels and it is the interaction between the two which provides the motivating forces for my art activity.

The working process advances on the basis of rational decisions which, in their turn, determine the physical limitations and the form of the work. I find that syntactical elements which in their identity are devoid of any specific emotional or other significance, and which are therefore in some measure anonymous, are those which are best suited to my intent. For practical purposes this has meant a frequent use of the square, the cube, and of numerical arrays which embody the concept of 'fourness'. In using colour, I also avoid the purely subjective and emotional, by employing colour as an element within a rational system devised for its distribution.

In this, as in other work, the organisational ethic is self evident, and the principles of permutation, transformation, rotation, or whatever, which have been used to activate the work, are there to be retrieved by the spectator. The ensuing dialogue based on objectivity rather than subjectivity, rationality rather than irrationality, in which the visual and conceptual are interactive, is intrinsic to the apprehension of the work and necessary to its analysis.

Roy Johnston Artist

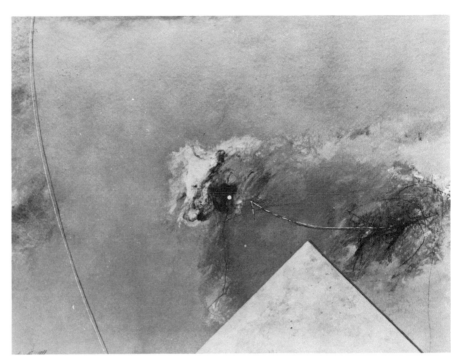

1. 'Ceremonial I' by Anthony O'Carroll

2. Roy Johnston

'The Map' by Jack B. Yeats

The artist who stakes his whole being comes from nowhere. And he has no brothers.

Should one expatiate then? On these fiercely immediate images that leave no place or time for comforting feats of skill. On this violence of need that unleashes the images and sends them flying beyond their horizons. On this vast inner reality where phantoms dead and alive, nature and void, all that never ends and all that will never be, unite in a single testimony, delivered once and for all.

Finally, on this supreme mastery that submits to the unmasterable, and trembles. No. Simply bow down, in wonderment.

Sam Beckett
'Hommage à Jack Yeats'

Jack B. Yeats by Sean O'Sullivan

James Joyce by Pavel Tchelitchev

"Chef Yeats, that master of the use of herbs
could raise mere stew to a glorious height:
pinch of saga, soupçon of philosophy,
carefully stirred in to get the flavour right,
and cook a poem around the basic verbs.
Our commis-chefs attend and learn the trade,
demoan the scraps of Gaelic that they know:
add to a simple Anglo-Saxon stock
Cuchulainn's marrow-bones to marinate,
a dash of O Rathaille simmered slow,
a glass of University hic-haec-hoc:
sniff and stand back and proudly offer you
the celebrated Anglo-Irish stew"

Michael Hartnett

won't you be an artist's moral
and pose in your nudies as a
local esthetic before voluble old
masters, introducing you, left to
right the party comprises, to
hogarths like Bottiselly and
Titteretto and Bergognese and
Coraggio with their extrahand
Mazzaccio, plus the usual bilker's
dozen of dowdycameramen.

James Joyce
from 'Finnegan's Wake'

W B Yeats and the Irish Theatre by Edmund Dulac

George Bernard Shaw by Sir John Lavery

Nobody can be better aware than
I am of the convenience to an
Irishman in England of being
able, by an occasional cunning
flourish of his nationality, to
secure all the privileges of a
harmless lunatic without
forfeiting the position of a
responsible member of society.

G B Shaw 1.2.1896

I never lived the literary life, or
belonged to a literary club; and
though I brought all my powers
unsparingly to the criticism of
fine arts, I never frequented their
social surroundings. My time
was fully taken up (when I was
not writing or attending
performances) by public
work. . . this training of
mine . . . has enabled me to
produce an impression of being
an extraordinarily clever, original
and brilliant writer, deficient only
in feeling, whereas the truth is
that though I am in a way a man
of genius. . .yet I am not in the
least 'brilliant' and not at all
ready or clever. If literary men
generally were put through the
mill I went through and kept out
of their stuffy little coteries,
where works of art breed in and
in until the intellectual and
spiritual product becomes
hopelessly degenerate, I should
have a thousand rivals more
brilliant than myself.

G B Shaw
Letter to Archibald
Henderson 30.6.1904

General Exhibitions

Punchestown Standing Stone

West of West

These monuments provide the opportunity to sample Ireland and its heritage in a most pure and even spiritual way. We have to think about the landscape of man, the way human beings created these spaces, organised materials and built such rich places which still exist to-day.

We think that some contemporary artists share a relationship with landscape which is close to man/ancient site/sculpture. A consideration of artistic thinking and not archaeology or history perhaps provides the insight necessary, if an understanding of these places is sought for.

Nigel Rolfe

The natural perception of the
Irish country people preserves
their contacts with the spirits of
the land.

John Michell

Like dolmens round my
childhood, the old people.

John Montague

Stack of Turf

Wood Quay occupation 5.6.79

Gaming Board excavated at Wood Quay, Dublin

'I recall here the riots in Dublin at
the time of the first performance
of the "Playboy of the Western
World" and Yeats telling the
Abbey audience they had
disgraced themselves. We
would disgrace ourselves again
if we allowed the building-over
of this site to occur.'

Michael O'Leary
Labour Party, Deputy Leader
18/9/79

Weavers very often turn labourers, which is attributed to so many being, contrary to law, bound apprentices for two years instead of five; by which means they are bad hands, and can do only the coarsest work. As to health, from the sedentary life, they rarely change their profession for that. They take exercise of a different sort, keeping packs of hounds, every man one, and joining; they hunt hares: a pack of hounds is never heard, but all the weavers leave their looms, and away they go after them by hundreds. This much amazed me, but assured it was very common. They are in general apt to be licentious and disorderly; but they are reckoned to be rather oppressed by the country uses for road, etc, which are not of general use. They are in general very bad farmers, being but the second attention, and it has a bad effect on them, stiffening their fingers and hands, so that they do not return to their work so well as they left it.

Arthur Young
'A Tour in Ireland' July 1776

Top, Irish Patchwork

Right, Aran Men c. 1910

Dublin Opinion, December 1932

A MODEST PROPOSAL.

The President of our Society of Architects has called attention to the fact that there is at the present day no distinctively Irish type of architecture, that the buildings which are being run up all over the place are merely copies of buildings in England and elsewhere, and do not reflect the genius of our race.

Something must be done to remedy this, and as a commencement, we submit our artist's conception of a terrace of middle-class houses which can be constructed at low cost and which would strike a distinctively National note. Apart entirely from aesthetic considerations, there is something about the "round tower" model which renders it peculiarly suitable to modern conditions. It is almost impossible for bailiffs to enter, or for writs to be served without the co-operation of the tenant, and the circular walls present an unsolvable problem to cats.

Plan of Ground Floor (15 feet in diameter).

Plan of First Floor (15 feet in diameter).

Plan of Second Floor (10 feet in diameter).

NOTE. Plans for Labourers' Cottages built on a smaller scale, and with less ornamental roofs may be inspected at our offices.

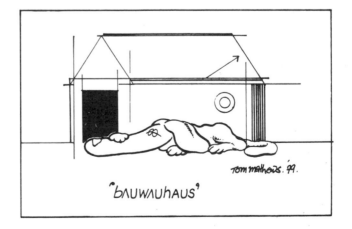

"bauwauhaus"

1.

Even the very lame and blind
If trump or bagpipe they do hear
In dancing posture do appear.

Moffet
'Irish Hudibras' 1728

Pípaí, fidlí, fir cea gail,
cnámfhir agus cuisleannaig
(bagpipes, fiddles, men of no
valour, bone players and pipe
blowers) were part of the
entertainment provided at the
Fair of Carmann, according to a
poet writing around the middle
of the eleventh century.

Breandán Breathnach
'Folk Music & Dances of Ireland'

'And he heard it
High up in the air
A piper, piping away,
And never was piping so sad
And never was piping so gay.'

W B Yeats
from 'The Hosts of the Air'

2.

The house was lifted by two
pillared wings
Out of its bulk of solid chisellings
And flashed across the chestnut-
marshalled lawn,
A few lit windows on a bullock
bawn.

Michael Hartnett
'A Visit to Castletown House'

Time passed. The pale white
privet flowers vanished from the
hedges. By mid-October only the
blackberries remained. By then
the swallows had gone too.
Before the end of the month, the
bush bearing privet berries had
begun to fade and wither after
the blossoms. Over Castletown
front gate the rain streamed
down the eroding forms of the
sphinxes, down their simple
faces, tautened ribs, down the
gate columns embellished with
bas-relief targe and drooping
garland of ivy. The leaves on the
lime trees had turned the colour
of copper. Water streamed down
the walls of Christ's Church
within the estate grounds, down
the spears of the gate. She stood
there, facing the open gate,
looking along the avenue of
limes darkening in the rain.

Aidan Higgins
Langrishe, Go Down'

Dr. Boris by Martyn Turner

No Country for Old Men

That is no country for old men. The young
in one another's arms, birds in the trees –
Those dying generations – at their song

W B Yeats: Sailing to Byzantium (1927)

This exhibition sets the social context for the artistic events of the Festival. By emphasising the complexity and even the contradictions of the social background in which contemporary Irish art is produced, we try to create a sense, not just of Ireland, but of the many different Irelands inhabited by those inside the country and perceived by those outside.

That there might be many different Irelands was clear in the heady decades at the start of this century, when men and women of very different traditions, following desperate visions, fought in their different ways for an independent Ireland. For some, that Ireland was to be socialist; for many more it was to be egalitarian. For some, it was to be Irish in language and culture, yet internationalist in outlook; for some, Catholic yet non-sectarian; for some, able to provide the plain necessities of life for all its people, yet committed to higher things than material growth. . .

The Free State which emerged after 1922 seemed to bear little resemblance to these visions. While formal political independence had been gained for twenty six of the thirty counties of Ireland, economic and cultural dependence continued. The destruction of colonial rule in the South had done little to promote a more equal society; the running sore of emigration worsened as the decades wore on. The poverty of the South was hard to defend against the vaunted British standard of living of the North; and both North and South of the Border politics were dominated by the parochial and sectarian concerns of an introverted bourgeoisie. From the thirties to the fifties, Ireland seemed frozen into the stereotype of the depressed peripheral region.

In the last twenty years, however, Ireland has changed perhaps more dramatically than any other country in Europe. Rapid economic growth and industrialisation in the Republic, and the decline of established industries in the North, have helped to reverse traditional images of the two societies in recent years. At the same time, the young age and burgeoning growth of the Republic's population suggest similarities with dependent Third World economies, while in terms of social structure and living standards, both North and South remain part of the periphery of Europe. Cultural production in Ireland is also 'dependent', in that it remains largely shaped by foreign influences. In educational and other spheres, foreign intellectuals and experts play a significant role, and the Irish cultural market is increasingly absorbed into a wider Anglo-American system.

External cultural influences are nevertheless internalised within Ireland in specific ways. This theme is explored in our first exhibit, which analyses the recent expansion of rock music in Belfast and Dublin. Rock music is hardly part of a conventional image of Ireland. For this reason, its sudden institutionalisation in these two cities is indicative of recent social changes — of urbanisation and of shifts in demographic and class structure. The explosion of rock music in Dublin also gives rise to questions about the traditional images of North and South: is the South, in some respects at least, now more 'modern' than the North?

The same question is addressed in the next exhibit, which examines the new industries in the South and the run-down of traditional industries both North and South. The context of the new Irish industrialisation is the growth of the transnational corporation and the specific political situation of post-World War II Europe, while the political organisation of the Republic's economic miracle has been carried out by a novel form of state apparatus, the Industrial Development Authority. The section concludes by examining the new 'domestic' bourgeoisie in the South and the political challenge posed by an emergent labour movement.

But in spite of the growth of industrialisation, the conventional image of Ireland remains that of a rural society. The next section, therefore, explores recent social changes in rural Ireland particularly the agricultural sector. The traditional description of Irish society is as a 'peasant' society, but this is both historically and geographically incomplete. 'Modernisation' has been imposed on agriculture through state policy, leading to very different responses from different groups of farmers, particularly in the context of membership of the European Economic Community.

The production of different images of Ireland within different newspapers forms the focus of the next section, which also involves some issues in contemporary Irish politics. Starting with the relationship between leading newspapers and Irish political parties, this examines firstly how two particular papers (The Irish Press and the Irish Independent) produce in their writing different 'real Irelands', and secondly how sectarianism is produced by different newspapers in the North. It concludes with the British media, and shows how their 'practical Unionism' occludes any awareness of the specific nature of Ireland by their subsumption of it under British liberal categories.

Two minorities within the Republic have had an influence on the shaping of society quite disproportionate to their size or strength — Irish speakers, and Protestants. We look at trends in the maintenance of the Irish language, government linguistic policy, the anglicisation of Gaeltacht areas and the use of Irish in social mobility. This is counterbalanced by an examination of the disappearance of a clearly defined Protestant community, and the effects of the symbiotic relationship between Protestant and Catholic church leaders. This section ends with a comparison of denominational groups North and South, stressing the different distribution of Protestants in the two states.

The next section focuses on women in Ireland, and asks how their position has changed in recent years. It begins with two contrasting aspects of women's life in small-town Ireland — the woman working in secretarial employment in Dublin and returning 'to the country' at weekends, the woman staying and working (in domestic labour) at home. It then examines three influences on women: religious imagery, male censorship, 'modern' alternatives. It concludes with 'the working woman's world' of factory work in Dublin, the success of middle class women's political organisations and the contrasting failure of the trade unions to mobilise women effectively.

The final section examines the meaning of 'Ireland' for different groups inside and out-side the country. We look at conflicts around contrasting notions of what Ireland should be — one state or two. Catholic or secular, issues in education, planning and environment, the im-ages of a rural arcadia and a modern industrial state. In many cases both issues and images turn out to derive from imported ideologies; will there be anything peculiarly 'Irish' about how they are resolved? From the 1930s to the 1950s many thousands of Irish people had to leave their country to search for jobs and opportunities elsewhere, taking with them an im-age of the homeland which remained with them unchanged throughout their experiences overseas. If they returned today, would they recognise in it their own 'Ireland'? The old country has become young again, but perhaps they would find that its transformation makes it now 'no country for old men'.

The exhibition is produced by Brian Torode, Hilary Tovey and James Wickham, members of the Department of Sociology at Trinity College, Dublin, with research assistance from some of their students. Design is by Raymond Kyne.

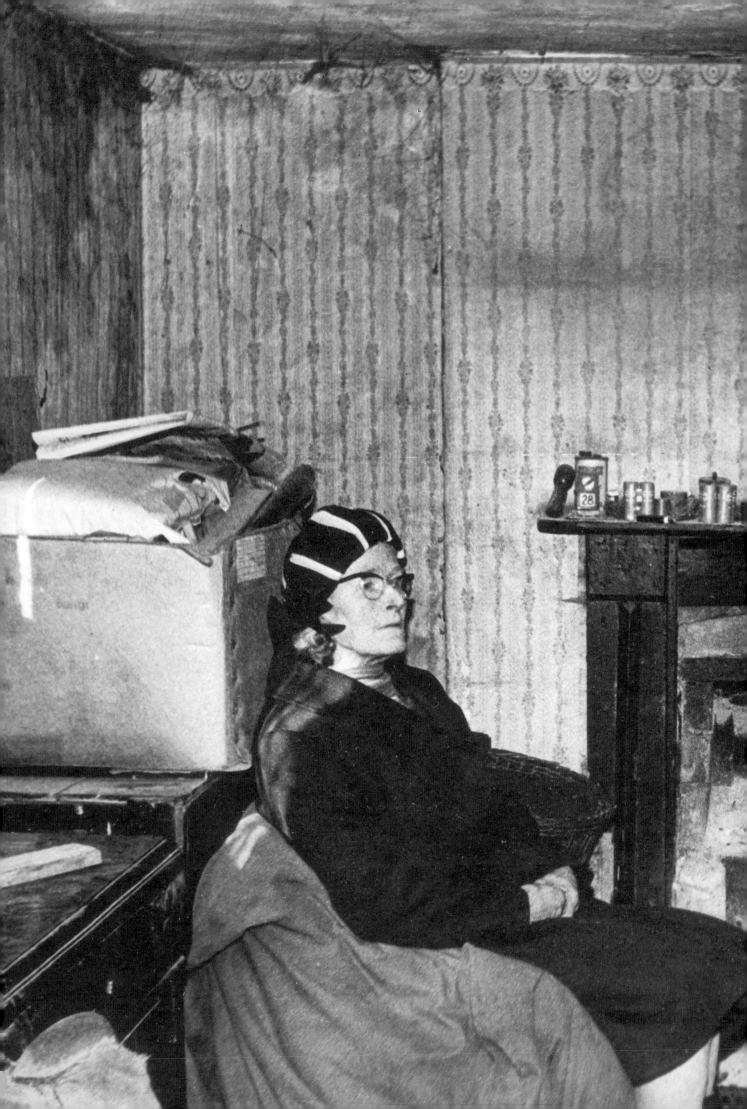

These people dressed up in their best clothes on hearing of the photographer's visit.

Above, landscape by John A. Davies

Aspects of Ireland
Ireland's Eye
Three Points of View

Photography

A Dying Art

'That day would skin a fairy —
A dying art, she said.
Not many left of the old trade
Redundant and remote, they age
Gracefully in dark corners
With lamplighters, sailmakers
And native Manx speakers.

And the bone-handled knives
with which
They earned their bread? My
granny grinds
Her plug tobacco with one to
this day'

Derek Mahon

Tony Murray

Question: Can a photograph be a work of art?

Answer: A photograph is a disposition of sensible matter and may be so disposed for an aesthetic end but it is not a human disposition of sensible matter.

Therefore it is not a work of art.

James Joyce

At Puck Fair, Rod Tuach

Tony Murray

Carrownisky, Co. Mayo, Rod Tuach

The Island

'Remarks
From old watchers who live at
their window-panes
And the tongues of the craw-
thumpers licking
the scabs of their
spite'

Desmond O Grady

RTE Academica String Quartet
RTE Singers with Veronica McSwiney
Northern Irish Musicians
John O'Conor
Bernadette Greevy with John O'Conor
Gerald Barry
Ulster Orchestra
RTE Symphony Orchestra
New Irish Chamber Orchestra
Geraldine O'Grady, Frank Patterson and
Eily O'Grady

Concerts

'Bodley is using his international and urban experience and involvement with ordinary "classical music" and also a deep historical knowledge and scholarship to approach a synthesis. It is characteristic that he extends the technique of a modern Irish harp by writing serious almost avant-garde music for it'

Charles Acton
'Irish Music & Musicians'

Recent Irish Music

In general the influences on Irish composers from the 1930s onward come from three sources: English 20th century music; Continental 20th century music and Irish folk-music. All three elements naturally do not affect *all* Irish composers and it goes without saying that within the general frame-work a very high degree of diversity obtains. The overall impression of Irish composition of the last fifty years is one of very great diversity of styles, a certain liveliness, and a willingness to try different approaches. On the whole the influence of English music has been much less than one might expect. Most of those Irish composers who studied in England also studied on the continent, or took an interest in Continental musical developments. The continental musical influence on Irish music takes two main forms: tonal modern style and 'avant-garde' style. This last style (or group of styles) began to influence Irish composers in the early 1960s. It has continued to influence some Irish composers, though even here there is a considerable diversity of approach.

The matter of the use of material from Irish traditional music is even more vexed. Though traditional music in the broad sense is extensively played and listened to in Ireland, its main use in Irish compositions has been on the style of melodic line adapted in many tonal compositions. The influence is most often shown in melodic forms of movement that derive directly from traditional Irish music. Some more recent developments however do make very direct use of original material drawn from the traditional Irish ornamental musical style. All of these various influences, Continental, Irish, English, make up the totality of contemporary Irish music. Is there a specifically Irish style of musical composition? Viewing the overall picture one might be inclined to say yes. However doubtless some Irish composers would adapt the attitude of Sir Boyle Roche: 'If the question were put to me, sir, I'd answer at once boldly in the affirmative – NO!'

Seoirse Bodley

. . .Unfortunately, Mozart's music is not everybody's affair when it comes to conducting. His scores do not play themselves by their own physical weight, as many heavy modern scores do. When a sense of duty occasionally urges the Philharmonic or the Crystal Palace to put the G minor or the E flat or the Jupiter symphony in the bill, the band, seeing nothing before them but easy diatonic scale passages and cadences smoothly turned on dominant discords, races through with general effect of a couple of Brixton schoolgirls playing one of Diabelli's pianoforte duets. The audience fidgets during the allegro; yawns desperately through the andante; wakes up for a moment at the minuet, finding the trio rather pretty; sustains itself during the finale looking forward to the end; and finishes by voting me stark mad when I speak of Mozart as the peer of Bach and Wagner, and in his highest achievements, the manifest superior of Beethoven.

G B Shaw
'Music in London'

RTE Academica String Quartet

John O'Conor

New Irish Chamber Orchestra

Portrait of Bernadette Greevy by Robert Ballagh

. . . .this nation of befuddled paddies, whose sole musical tradition is bound up with blind harpers, tramps with home-made fiddles, Handel in Fishhandel street, John McCormack praising our airport, and no street in the whole capital named after John Field.

Flann O Brien

Laſt Wedneſday one Mc-Gennis was hanged at Kilmainham, for returning from Tranſportation.

Laſt Monday Patrick Fleming, Daniel Tully, Patrick Tully and Dirby Tracy, were executed at the Curragh of Kildare, and hanged in Chains, for robbing a Cabbin belonging to four old Brothers named Dowling, at Newhal near Naas, and cutting three of them moſt cruelly, and the fourth Brother who had been a-bread, and coming home at that Time, they ſtabbed in three Places with a Hanger, of which he inſtantly died, and carried off 20 l. and other Goods, the 26th of September laſt, as formerly mentioned in this Paper. They all confeſſed this Fact, and ſome other Crimes, and behaved themſelves very penitently at the Place of Execution.

Yeſterday Mr. Handell's new Grand Sacred Oratorio, called, The MESSIAH, was rehearſed at the Muſick-Hall in Fiſhamble Street, to a moſt Grand, Polite and crouded Audience ; and was performed ſo well, that it gave univerſal Satisfaction to all preſent ; and was allowed by the greateſt Judges to be the fineſt Compoſition of Muſick that ever was heard, and the ſacred Words as properly adapted for the Occaſion.

N.B. At the Deſire of ſeveral Perſons of Diſtinction, the above Performance is put off to Tueſday next The Doors will be opened at Eleven, and the Performance begin at Twelve.

Many Ladies and Gentlemen who are well-wiſhers to this Noble and Grand Charity for which this Oratorio was compoſed, requeſt it as a Favour, that the Ladies who honour this Performance with their Preſence would be pleaſed to come without Hoops, as it will greatly encreaſe the Charity, by making Room for more Company.

The Committee of the Muſical Society are deſired to meet on Wedneſday the 14th Inſt. at their Room in Fiſhamble Street, at ſix a Clock in the Evening, to conſider of matters relating to the good of the Society.

Imported 70 Tons of Corn.

Detail from Freeman's Journal

99

Gerald Barry

. . .For the visitor it was the new Irish Music that provided the main focus of interest. And it was perhaps indicative of a much more general under-current that several of the more stimulating scores were by composers like Raymond Deane and Gerald Barry who have worked extensively on the Continent with Stockhausen and the latter also with Kagel. . . .

. . .Indeed Gerald Barry's setting for speaker cello and piano from a 10th century Japanese diary in his 'Things that Gain by Being Painted was one of the real discoveries of the festival, full of teasing humour and impeccable in its comic timing of work and musical gesture. . .

. . .Perhaps by 1980 these same young composers will have found a new courage that will enable them to add their own lustre to this most welcoming and agreeable festival.

Robert Henderson
on the 1977 Dublin Festival
of 20th Century Music

The working man. . .knows well enough that society is not divided into 'animated clothes-pegs' on the one hand and lovers of Beethoven in ligatured corduroys on the other. For Beethoven purposes society is divided into people who can afford to keep a piano and go to operas and concerts, and people who cannot. . . . .*The* musical public is the shilling public, by which I mean the people who can afford to pay not more than a shilling a once a week or so for a concert without going short of more immediately necessary things. . . .professional and business men of musical tastes who work hard, and whose brains are of such a quality that a Beethoven symphony is a recreation to them, instead of an increased strain on their mental powers, are keen patrons of music, though, in outward seeming they belong to the 'animated clothes-pegs' section.

G B Shaw 31.5.1889

The admirers of Brahms had a succulent treat at the Richter concert last week. His German Requiem was done from end to end; and done quite well enough to bring out all his qualities. What those qualities are could have been guessed by a deaf man from the mountainous tedium of the unfortunate audience, who yet listened with a perverse belief that Brahms is a great composer, and the performance of this masterpiece of his an infinitely solemn and important function. I am afraid that this delusion was not confined to those who, having found by experience that good music bores them, have rashly concluded that all music that bores them must be good. . . .

G B Shaw
'Music in London'

All softly playing
With head to the music bent
And fingers straying
Upon an instrument.

from 'Chamber Music'
by James Joyce

The Chieftains
De Danann
The Dubliners
Andy Irvine
Christy Moore
Planxty
Stockton's Wing
Irish and London
based musicians

Traditional Music

Their Sunday is the most leisure
day they have, on which they use
all manner of sport; in every field
a fiddle and the lasses footing it
till they are all of a foam, and
grow infinitely proud with the
blear eye of affection her
sweetheart casts on her feet as
she dances to a tune, or no tune,
played on an instrument that
makes a worse noise than a key
upon a gridiron.

Richard Head
'The Western Wonder'   1674

Seamus Ennis

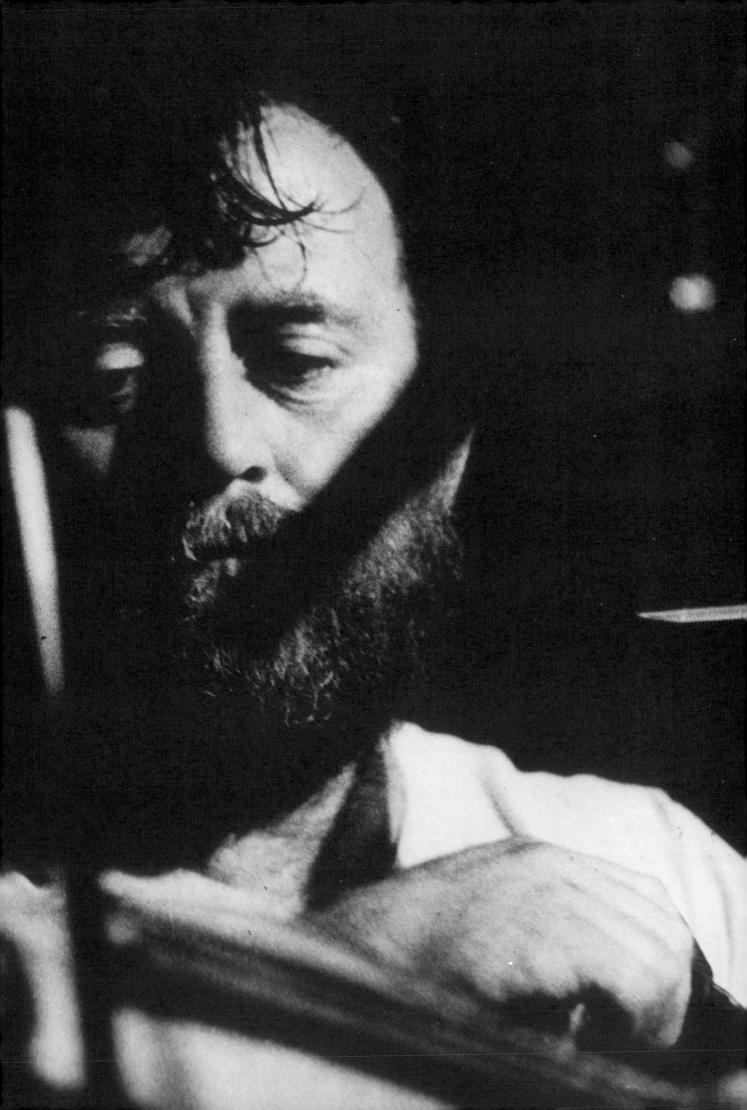

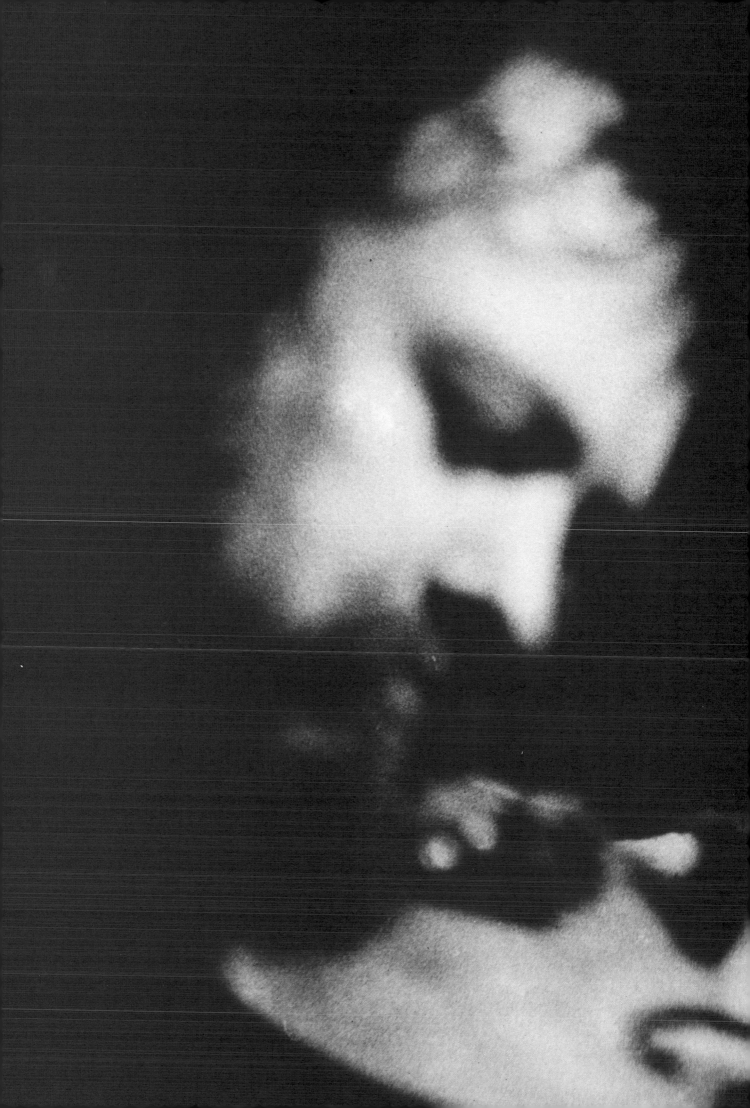

Neansaí Mhíle Grá

A Neansaí mhíle ghrá. a bhruinneal tá gan smál,
Go bhfeice mise 'ntádh 'gus an séan ort
Ba ghile do dhá láimh ná cur geal na trá
Ná 'n eala 'sí a' snámh ar an Eirne.
Ba ghlaise liom do shúil ná braon beag de'n drúcht,
Is binne liomsa thú ná na treadaí;
's mur 'n-éalaíonn tusa liomsa titfhidh mise i leanndubh
Is cuirfinn in san chill do dhiaidh mé.

Love song sung by Alphonsus Mac a Bhaird
of Teelin, Co. Donegal.
Recorded by Clannad.

Rock/New Wave

'That's my broken arrow
Going down those streets so
small and narrow
in the evenin
Just before the Sunday six bells
chime
six bells chime. . .

Van Morrison
'Beside You
from Astral Weeks

Van Morrison

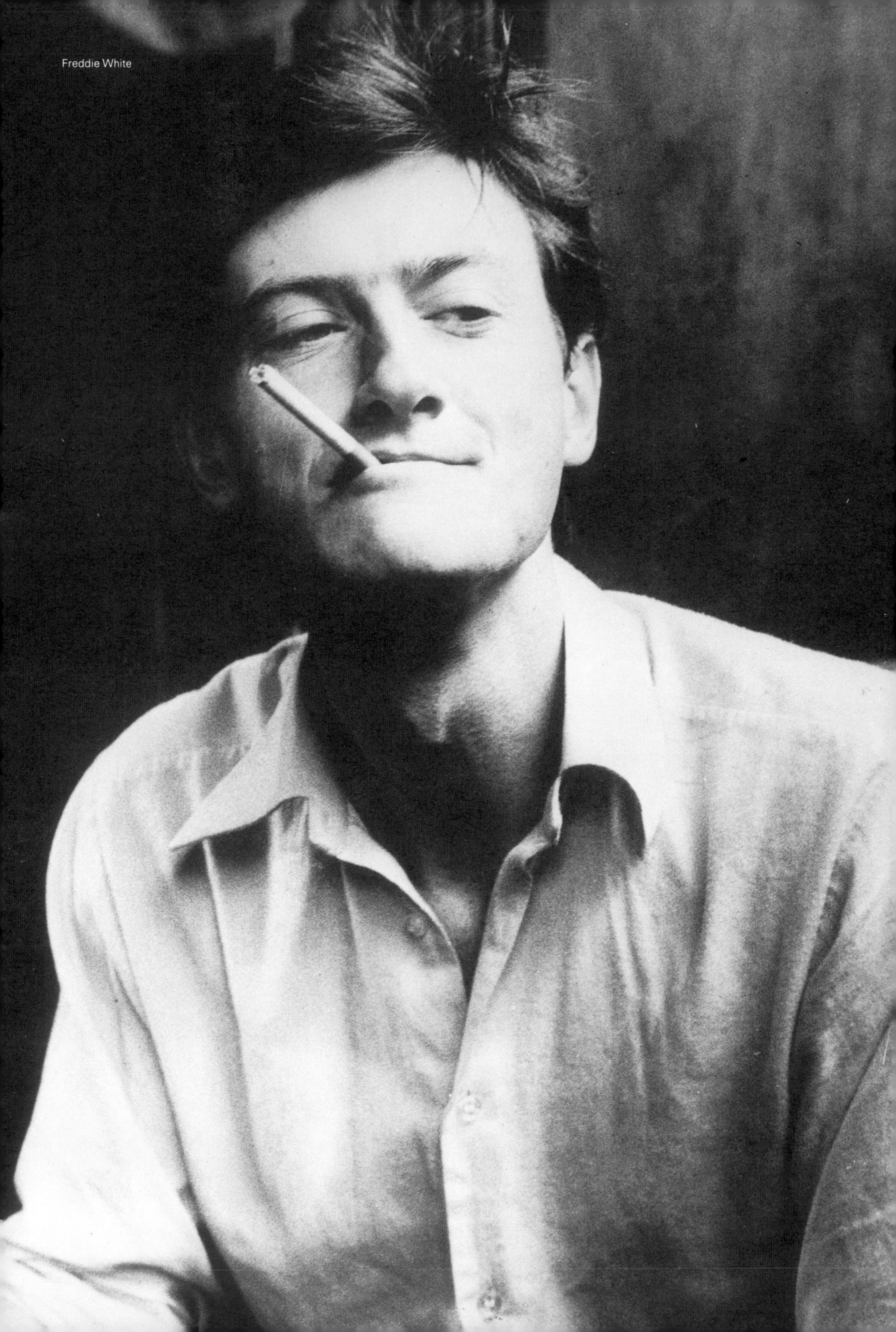
Freddie White

'And you know you gotta go
On a train from Dublin up to
Sandy Row
Throwing pennies at the bridges
down below
In the rain, hail, sleet and snow.'

Van Morrison
'Madame George'
from Astral Weeks

Guggi and Gavin of the Virgin Prunes

Rory Gallagher

Phil Lynott

Protex

U-2

Johnny Fean and Eamonn Carr of Horslips

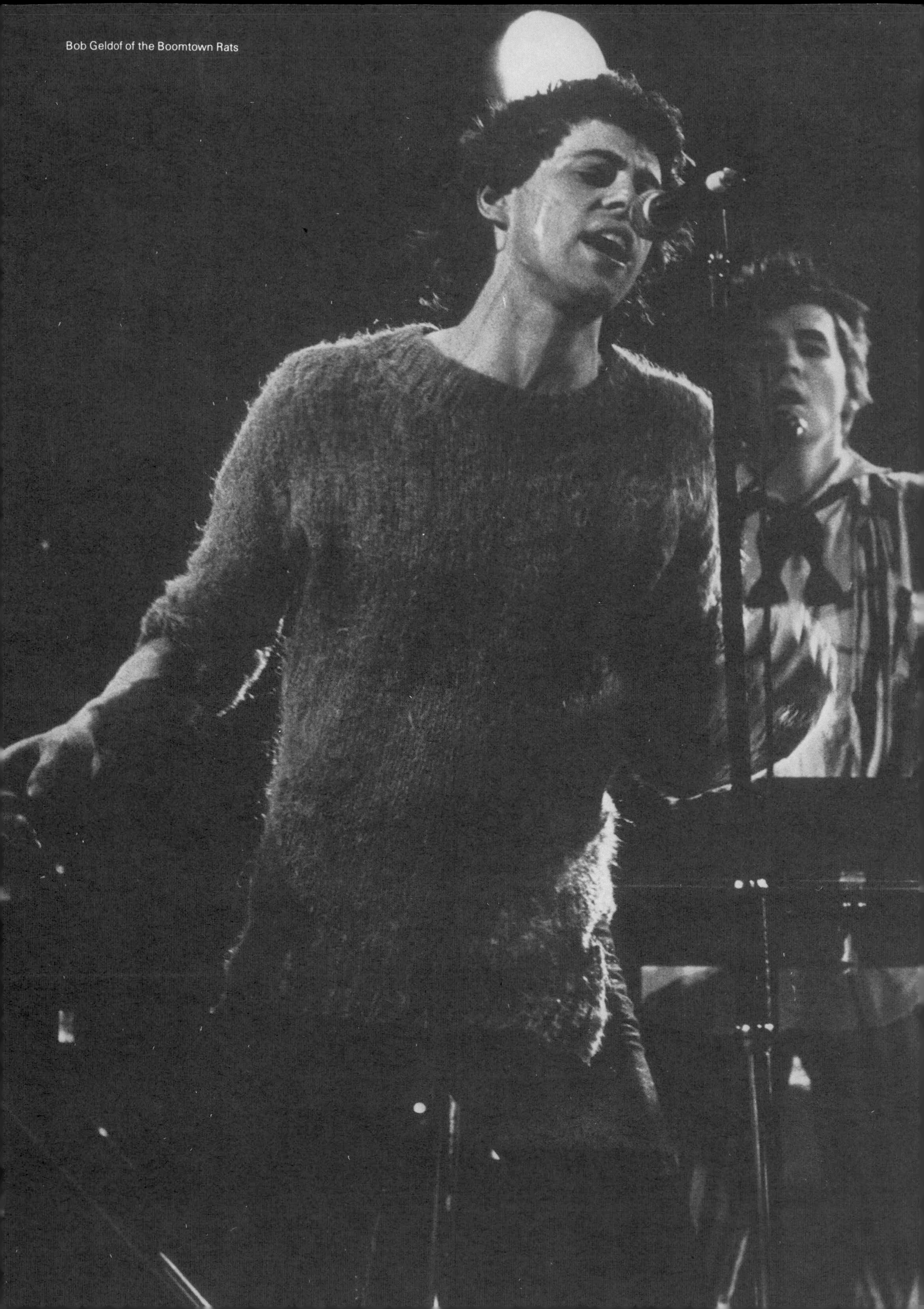
Bob Geldof of the Boomtown Rats

Noel Kelehan Quintet
Louis Stewart Quartet

Jazz

Brian Dunning

I don't think anybody can
master the art of jazz. . . I'm
only scratching the surface.

Brian Dunning

Keith Donald

The Louis Stewart Quartet

He heard the radio crackle over the sound of falling water and heard a rapid-fire succession of notes that seemed to spring from the falling water, that amazed him, so much faster than his father ever played, but slow behind it all, melancholy, like a river. He came out of the toilet and stood listening with his father. Who is that, he asked his father. Then he heard the continuity announcer say the name Charlie Parker and saw his father staring at some point between the wooden table and the wooden holiday-home floor.

Neil Jordan
'Night in Tunisia'

Sitting po-faced under a sepia photograph of giraffes in the East African bush, I would mentally add jazz to Bolshevism and the lower classes (Spurni profanum vulgus) as things I was in favour of.

George Melly

Louis Stewart

Irish Writing Today
Writers at the Round House

Literature

Drawing by Louis Le Brocquy

Patrick Kavanagh: Drawing by Sean O'Sullivan

He had the knack of making men
feel
As small as they really were
Which meant as great as God
had made them
But as males they disliked his air.
O he was a proud one
Fol dol the di do,
He was a proud one
I tell you.

Patrick Kavanagh
from 'If Ever You Go To Dublin
Town'

'Gaels!', he said, 'it delights my Gaelic heart to be here today speaking Gaelic with you at this Gaelic feis in the centre of the Gaeltacht. May I state that I am a Gael. I'm Gaelic from the crown of my head to the soles of my feet – Gaelic front and back, above and below. . .we are all Gaelic Gaels of Gaelic lineage. . . I myself have spoken not a word except Gaelic since the day I was born – just like you – and every sentence I've ever uttered has been on the subject of Gaelic. There is nothing in this life so nice and so Gaelic as truly true Gaelic Gaels who speak in true Gaelic Gaelic about the truly Gaelic language.'

Flann O Brien
'The Poor Mouth'

'A Ghaela', adúirt sé, 'cuireann sé gliondar ar mo chroí Gaelach a bheith anseo inniu ag caint Ghaeilge libhse ar an gheis Ghaelach seo i lár na Gaeltachta. Ní miste dom a rá gur Gael mise. Táim Gaelach ó m'bhathais go bonn mo choise – Gaelach thoir, thiar, thuas agus thios . . . Gaeil Ghaelacha de shliocht Ghaelach is ea an t-iomlán againn . . . Níor labhair mise (ach oiread libh féin) aon fhocal ach Gaeilge ón lá rugadh me agus, rud eile, is fán nGaeilge amháin a bhí gach abairt dár ndúras riamh . . . Níl aon ní ar an domhan chomh deas nó chomh Gaelach le fíorGhaeil fíorGhaelacha a bhíonn ag caint fíorGhaeilge Gaelaí i dtaobh na Gaeilge fíorGhaelaí. . .'

Flann O Brien
'An Béal Bocht'

"The man outside the beauty parlour"

I'm an outsider. That's a cosy place
to walk in out of the windy streets and sit.
Some gorgeous women shoulder the swing door,
like horses, groomed and shining for great races,
hair set elaborately, and tastefully
distorted. Useless for running in, I'd say,
or making love; but a joy, a real eyeful.
You'd easy roar with laughter or start to cheer
as we did at the Jubilee — do at poodles
or the crazy sculptured hedges on big estates.
Which, incidentally, I want in public parks
when the revolution comes. The workers' duty,
to foster comic skills of gardeners. . .
and beauty parlours, comrades, and high couture.

James Simmons

I am Ulster, my people an abrupt
people
Who like all the spiky consonants
in speech
And think the soft ones cissy;
who dig
The k and t in orchestra, detect
sin
In sinfonia, get a kick out of
Tin cans, fricatives, staccato talk,
Anything that gives or takes
attack
Like Micks, Tagues, tinkers' gets,
Vatican.

W R Rodgers
from the Epilogue to
'The Character of Ireland'

Ulster — old decency
And Old Bushmills
Soda Farl, strong tea,
New rope, rock salt, kale plants,
Potato-bread and Woodbine.
Wind through the concrete vents
Of a border check-point.

Séamus Heaney

'Just to gaze at something rather
than to argue.
I think that whatever kind of
poetry I can write,
I'm probably better at something
more like a gaze.'

Séamus Heaney

Foxford, Co. Mayo

Irish seems to me a splendid
vehicle for certain subjects and
excellent for what I call the hard
stuff. When it comes to more
subtle intimations I wonder if
there is enough verbal variety
available for the artist.

Sean O Faolain

Daoine Bochta

Bhí fuaim na mara ag
filleadh go borb trí
dorchadas ciúin an
    mhaidneacháin. . .
fuaim fhada bhriste
ag únfairt ar ghaineamh
geal na trá.
. . .Cothrom na talún
dudhaite, faoi shuan.

Poor Folk

The sound of the sea
grumbled through the
calm darkness of
    the dawn. . .
a long broken sound
wallowing on the
white sand of the beach.
. . .The form of the earth
slept, covered in
    darkness.

Liam O Flaherty
writing in English and
Irish from a short story
published in 1937

The Voyage of St Brendan

The Road's End

          . . . .Uncurling
Fern, white scut of *canavan,*
Spars of bleached bog fir jutting
From heather, make a landscape
So light in wash it must be learnt
Day after day, in shifting detail,
Out to the pale Sperrins
          . . . .Like shards
Of a lost culture, the slopes
Are strewn with cabins, deserted
In my lifetime. Here the older
People sheltered; the Blind
Nialls,
Big Ellen, who has been a Fair-
Day prostitute. The bushes
cramp
To the evening wind as I reach
The road's end.

John Montague
from 'The Rough Field'

Slate

Slate I picked from a nettle-bed
Had history, my neighbour said.

To quarry it, men had to row
Five miles, twelve centuries ago.

An inch thick, it hung watertight
Over monks' litany by
candlelight:

Till stormed by Viking raids, it
slipped.
Four hundred years overlapped.

Pirates found it and roofed a fort
A mile west, commanding the
port.

Red clawed choughs perched on
it saw
Guards throw priests to the sea's
jaw.

Repaired to succour James the
Shit
The battle of Aughrim shattered
it.

Through centuries of penal gale
Hedge-scholars sheltered where
it fell.

Pegged above a sea-wormed
rafter
It rattled over landlord's laughter.

Windy decades pined across
Barrack roof, rebellion, moss.

This week I paved my garden
path
With slate St Colman nailed on
lath.

Richard Murphy
from 'The Battle of Aughrim'

The Playboy of the Western World
the Irish Ballet Company
with the Chieftains

Ballet

This impulse to protect the
criminal is universal in the West.
It seems partly due to the
association between justice and
the hated English jurisdiction,
but more directly to the primitive
feeling of these people – who are
never criminals yet always
capable of crime – that a man
will not do wrong unless he is
under the influence of a passion
which is as irresponsible as a
storm on the sea. If a man has
killed his father, and is already
sick and broken with remorse,
they can see no reason why he
should be dragged and killed by
the law.

Such a man, they say, will be
quiet all the rest of his life, and if
you suggest that punishment is
needed as an example, they ask:
would anyone kill his father if he
was able to help it?'

J M Synge

West Cork Ballad

The Playboy of the Western World

Jimmy	He'll lick them yet!
Widow Quin	He'd lick them if he was running races with a score itself.
Mahon	Look at the mule he has, kicking the stars.
Widow Quin	There's a lep! He's fallen! He's mounted again! Faith, he's passing them all!
Jimmy	Look at him skelping her!
Philly	And the mountain girls hooshing him on!
Jimmy	It's the last turn! The post's cleared for them now!
Mahon	Look at the narrow place. He'll be into the bogs! (With a yell.) Good rider! He's through it again!
Jimmy	He's neck and neck!
Mahon	Good boy to him! Flames, but he's in! (Great cheering, in which all join.)

from 'The Playboy of the Western World' by J M Synge

The Playboy of the Western World

The Chieftains

Theatre: that stuffy
uncomfortable place of penance
in which we suffer so much
inconvenience on the slenderest
chance of gaining a scrap of food
for our starving souls.

G B Shaw
'Heartbreak House'

A Life
The Risen People
The Liberty Suit
The Man who boxed like John McCormack
The Keytag
Now you see him, Now you don't
The State of Emergency:
O Wilde and his mother
1980's Spit and Polish Girlie Show
and other events

An Damer theatre poster

Theatre

...the management of the Abbey Theatre have made a grave tactical mistake in introducing police into the theatre. It was a mistake to associate a theatre whose effort is to become a National Theatre with police protection.....the management of the Abbey Theatre have frankly used intimidation against intimidation...

Padraic Colum
Letter to Freeman's Journal
30.1.1907

'With regard to the disposal of these my body, mind and soul, I desire that they be burnt and placed in a paper bag and brought to the Abbey Theatre, Lr Abbey Street, Dublin, and without pause into what the great and good Lord Chesterfield calls the necessary house, where their happiest hours have been spent, on the right as one goes down into the pit, and I desire that the chain be there pulled upon them, if possible during the performance of a piece, the whole to be executed without ceremony or show of grief.'

Samuel Beckett
from 'Murphy'

If ever a revolution makes me Dictator, I shall establish a heavy charge for admission to our churches. But everyone who pays at the church door shall receive a ticket entitling him or her to free admission to one performance at any theatre he or she prefers. Thus shall the sensuous charms of the church service be made to subsidize the sterner virtue of the drama.

G B Shaw
'Heartbreak House'

Cyril Cusack and John Newman in 'The Plough and the Stars'.

John Kavanagh in 'The Silver Tassie'

Hugh Leonard: Portrait by Robert Ballagh

Item: I am not a frequenter of art exhibitions, having discovered from experience that there is rarely enough art and usually too much exhibitionism, but I confess that I went beetling along at some speed to see myself, warts and all, as portrayed by Mr Robert Ballagh. What I discover is not so much a portrait as a nocturne: it is, in fact, the fulfilment of the wish expressed by another Robert when he wrote: 'O wad some Pow'r the giftie gie us/To see oursels as others see us?'
Mr. Ballagh has seen me as a somewhat splenetic Philip Marlowe, looking to my left with a mixture of venom and suspicion, as if I had just decried a certain bearded and scungilaginous Corkman on the doorstep.

Hugh Leonard

1. Jack Doyle in street

2. Jack Doyle in shorts

'As I say, this encounter changed my life. Why? Well, in all my years in the force I have never been hit such a wallop by a human person. For all the punches I have dished out and for all the people who have fallen down stairs while in my custody, the worst form of retribution has been the exhalation of air from my bicycle tyres, by what I can only assume were pressure groups. I resolved, therefore, to follow the career of this Joseph Alphonsus Doyle. I discovered that he came of poor family and from a poor neighbourhood in County Cork, and that economic conditions forced him to emigrate like many another. Doyle, however, had a pleasing punch and a voice like a lark with singing lessons. When his chance came to drag himself out of the role historically bequeathed to members of his class, he grasped it with both hands. He was able to get on, unlike the majority of emigrants in a similar situation. He quickly made a name for himself, first as a boxer and then as a playboy. In the nineteen thirties he made a quarter of a million pounds. And spent it. He was feted by bourgeois society and became a symbol of the possibilities inherent in the capitalist ethic. He married Hollywood beauties and moved in what are termed the best circles. Bourgeois circles. But then, because his talent was based on the flimsiest of platforms, he foundered. His second wife left him and, unable to cope with his rapid descent, he took to the bottle in Dublin. He spent a time in Mountjoy Jail, he hit people when drunk. Worst of all, he hit a policeman in the execution of his duty. Bourgeois society closed its doors on him. He reverted to type.

Well. Looking into Doyle's history proved an educational experience for me. I became politically orientated. I painted my bicycle clips red. I cancelled my copy of the Beano. I now read Das Kapital in my tea-break. People still fall down the stairs while in my custody but they now do so on a rigid class basis.

Doyle was falling, but though he was falling he had not hit the ground yet. He gave up the drink, went back to England and settled a singing contract with an Irish club. But of course giving up the drink and staying off it are two individual and separate matters.'

Ian Macpherson
Speech by 'Policeman' from
'The Man who Boxed like John McCormack'

Conceptual – a vague, usually typed statement of intention to do something and then not do it, as it would not be a Conceptual then.

Nowhere is art more meaningless than in a modern contemporary art exhibition. Abstract sculpture had nothing to say out of its splendidly empty spaces, convexes, concavities, planes and lovely surfaces.

It is this element of mandatory excitement . . . the need to be 'impactful' . . . that renders the exhibition-orientated world of the modern movement irrelevant. The exhibition for its own sake will provide no permanent basis for a sane acceptance of the profession of the artist, or for a development of the Arts. What the public sees . . . is largely a circus. . .

The excesses of the modern movement: such as splintered boards nailed together, barbed wire coiled in a space, polythene enshrouding beaches, bandages, string-stretching, wire-pulling: the whole hideous charade. . . !

James McKenna

ROSC '77

I think it's all rubbish. I believe
that they're taking the people for
a ride, but then so long as I get
my few bob, what do I mind? . . .
makes a change. . .

Attendant

It is not enough, I feel, for the
artist to say it is up to ourselves
to find our own meaning from
his work. I think we have a right
to ask the artist what he is
getting at. We need a helping
hand to relate much of this
modern art to our own lives.

Mr Michael Collins
Former Lord Mayor of Dublin

I must confess that I do not
always understand or interpret
to my own satisfaction the works
of conceptual artists.

Mr Jack Lynch

From the film 'Young & Old'

Irish Cinema

Emtigon
Withdrawal
Down the Corner
Lament for Art O'Leary
Guests of the Nation
Willy Riley and the Colleen
Bawn
The Dawn
Exposure
A Child's Voice
Faithful Departed
Mise Eire
Saoirse?
On A Paving Stone Mounted
Poitin
Self Portrait with Red Car
Cloch
Rocky Road to Dublin
These Stones Remain
Wheels
Kinkisha
Yeats Country
Shell Shock Rock
Return to Glenescaul
Jack of all Maids
Pint of Plain
A week in the Life of Martin
Cluxton
Deeply regretted by . . . .
Its a Hard Oul' Station
Will to Win
Terminus: Gola Island
Down There
Three Funerals
Shankill Road
Young and Old
The Beneficiary
Croagh Patrick
Christmas Morning
From Time to Time
Conquest of Light
Flea Ceoil
Killer Swim

The Outsider's View

Home Soldier Home
Sense of Loss
People of Ireland
The Patriot Game
Ireland: Behind the Wire
Coilin and Platonida
Odd Man Out
Hennesy
Ryan's Daughter
Ulysses
Finnegan's Wake
Portrait of the Artist
as a Young Man
The Informer (Ford)
The Plough and the Stars
How Green Was My Valley
The Long Gray Line
The Rising of the Moon
Finian's Rainbow
A Fistful of Dynamite
Angels with Dirty Faces
The Last Hurrah
Man of Aran
Rory O'More
Donovan's Reef
Gentle Gunman
The Outsider

Cinema

Irish Cinema

From every viewpoint, an
unfortunate production, its
ethical 'message' was as
misguided as its technical
direction. . . Judging from this
film I would expect to be told that
Ireland today is a fit breeding
ground for anticlericism and
communism. . . To my mind
there can be only one answer
that besides being in the
'Pudovkin manner' this film is
also in the Soviet tradition.

The Catholic Standard, 1937
commenting on Tom Cooper's
'The Dawn'.

The Dawn

Irish Cinema has had a long and fruitful history which parallels developments in other parts of Europe. Unfortunately it has also tried to adopt styles, forms and production structures of wealthier countries. The most interesting Irish films have been made in an artisanal or independent production system. The imitative Hollywood/Elstree films made at Ardmore produced a crop of inferior commercial films. These films frequently lost money but more unfortunately they often reinforced an image of Ireland as a tourist facility and the Irish as quaint peasants rather than recording the rapid changes of Irish society over the past twenty years.

Irish Cinema, documentary and drama, began well before Independence. It developed with the struggle for Independence through feature length fiction films on historical themes and contemporary European cinema. In the economically bleak and inward-looking decades following Independence a few films were made which stand out, including 'Guests of the Nation' and 'The Dawn'.

Whilst discussions on an Irish film industry continued unabated in the 1940s and 1950s few were happy with the outcome. Ten years after its founding one leading Irish filmmaker described Ardmore as 'irrelevant'. The irrelevance of Ardmore to filmmakers who survived on sponsored documentaries in the 1960s and advertising work in the 1970s was magnified by their own exclusion from working on foreign productions.

A new crop of young filmmakers began to learn the slow, painful and frustrating method of amateur and 'independent' filmmaking. The first fruits of a desire to record the reality of Ireland's past and present was the landmark film 'Caoineadh Airt Ui Laoire' (Lament for Art O'Leary): an historical film with contemporary relevance; a film which also examines the film medium itself. Since then many more films have been made: 'Kinkisha', 'Down the Corner', 'Wheels', 'Poitin', 'Exposure', 'Withdrawal'. . .

The changes manifest in Irish society are showing expression in an explosion of native filmmaking. The independent Irish filmmaking tradition is bearing fruit though not within an imitative commercial cinema framework but within a scale which is possible and relevant to Irish society and the experience of Irish filmmakers. The Government have recently announced their intention to allocate £4 million to the development of an Irish film industry. Whether the direction shown by the Irish Cinema retrospective will be followed remains to be seen.

The seminar on March 1st will present different views on Ireland's film history and conflicting positions on what is required for the future. What is an *Irish* film? What type of film production structure is relevant to Ireland in the 1980s: 'Independent' or 'Imitative Commercial'?

Kevin Rockett

1. Young Cassidy

4. Ourselves Alone

2. Poitin

5. Guests of the Nation

3. Young Cassidy

6. A Child's Voice

'They journeyed down to where
the Abbey Theatre was standing,
surrounded by a multitude of
people forcing themselves to
hiss, blast, and boo the building.
A tiny building for a theatre,
thought Seán, two-storeyed, a
circular-topped window on each
side of a circular-topped door,
and three narrow, oblong
windows on the upper storey: a
glass-roofed awning jutting from
the main entrance over the
pathway, and, between the
storeys, THE ABBEY THEATRE in
bold letters on a panel
stretching from one end of the
building to the other. The three
of them went into a pub
opposite and furnished
themselves with a bottle of stout
apiece.

Seán O'Casey
from 'Drums under the Windows'

. . .Irish Censorship, both formal
and oblique, is strict, stupid and
pernicious.

Aidan Higgins
from 'Sight and Sound', 1951

When one appreciates the
character and ability of
(Eisenstein) it will be obvious
that any film made by him must
be treated as deadly poison by
Christian nations. Here in
Ireland, where practically
everyone is a politician and
political opinions have caused so
much senseless division
amongst the masses, with
consequent distrust of
Governments, it is no longer a
joke to assert: 'Whatever it is, if
it's against the Government I'm
for it'. Yet Potemkin glorifies that
doctrine.

Catholic Standard, 1936

1. Saoirse

2. Saoirse: Michael Collins

3. Cathal Black directing 'Our Boys'

They (the Irish) like big spectacles, musicals and drama with meaty situations. They won't stand for hokum.

Paramount's Dublin manager

The screening of 'Battleship Potemkin' is the thin edge of the wedge, preparatory to the introduction of more advanced Communistic doctrine by film.

Catholic Standard, 1936

There is a tradition of violent action even in such a matter of showing motion pictures which are considered objectionable by persons in audiences. The actual cases of serious audience trouble, even over a period of twenty years, are few in number. But exhibitors and distributors who have been in business any considerable length of time can recall cases when the objectionable film was taken out and publicly burnt.

Most of these occurrences were concerned with pictures held to be pro-British. But that has not applied in all cases. For example, an exhibitor told the writer that years ago one of the Morton Johnson African adventures was seized at the theatre and destroyed by private individuals.

Film trade paper, 1943

1. Barry Fitzgerald

2. Man of Aran

3. Odd Man Out

The Outsiders' View

Irish people are very sensitive to how they have been represented. The sensitivity is understandable in that the histories of drama, cartoons, television, fiction and film have almost exclusively depicted a stereotypical caricature that is felt to be at best erroneous, at worst insulting. The difference between British and American cinemas' representation of the Irish is often only one of themes or intensity, not of pertinence. Irish people's reaction to Ireland's representation abroad is one of amusement and benign resignation mixed with a feeling that ignorance reflected in the inaccuracy of the images is far from irrelevant.

In British cinema the depiction of Irish history is riddled with those inaccuracies, irrelevancies as well as gross simplifications. The surprising thing about British cinema's view of Ireland is how few films with Irish themes have been made despite the 'special relationship' which has existed between the two countries for so long. Film, though, is not the only medium where the ignoring of Ireland has been practised.

Television, whether situation comedy, (with its repetitive Irish jokes), current affairs, (the absence of a history of Ireland which could set English viewers bewilderment at Irish events in context), drama, (few made), or documentary, (when was the last time you saw a British TV documentary about the South?), leave a lot to be desired.

In America, the films of John Ford most popularly and consistently dealt with Ireland. Ford's films, at least on the surface, present either a quaint peasant life with a brogue language or an 'odd' view of Irish history and social organisations. Irish actors and actresses who emigrated to Hollywood have usually gone along with this depiction. In American cinema Irish men are most often represented as priests, policemen, politicians and (re)-publicans. The women are seen as stern, domineering mothers or rebellious 'girls', (wild Irish roses/colleens), who finally succumb to the 'charms' of the man to take her 'rightful place' as wife and mother.

The series of seminars organised in conjunction with these screenings will attempt to look past the surface meanings. They will try to introduce critical languages which will help in understanding these stereotypes and clarify the, often, gross distortions.

Kevin Rockett

The Rising of the Moon

. . . .if American studios must produce Irish stories, such stories should be true to character, and the actors should be Irish, or at least trained in the brogue, if a brogue is found to be necessary. The 'Bowery cum Irish brogue' is said to irritate. . . .The citizens of this country are said to detest what is known as the 'stagey Irish', usually depicted as a buffoon, a likeable but brainless sort of individual, It has been suggested that religious scenes should be avoided if they are not totally necessary to productions. The picture should give no indication to the audience as to whether the Irish character is Catholic or Protestant, and the scriptwriter should avoid putting into the mouth of the Irish character such expressions as 'begorrah', 'more power to your elbow', and a lot of 'sickening blarney'. The type of film is probably not as important here as the featured players. Musicals, action pictures, and comedies (provided the latter are not too sophisticated) are special favourites. Colour films have a strong appeal.

US Embassy reports, 1943

Lectures
Seminars

The Future of a Different Past

Two conceptions of Ireland and her problems can be identified in contemporary British thinking; conceptions that have been shared by some of the Irish since the sixties. The first might be called the *modernization* approach which views Ireland as backward in its relation to the ideal of a developed economy and polity, and analyses the blockages to that development. Blockages like the Church, nationalist ideology and agrarian dominance then provide an explanation of backwardness. The second conception, the *radical* approach, is that neo-colonial (and colonial in relation to the North) oppression explains the distorted structure of the Irish States.

The seminar series is built around a challenge to these dominant theses. It examines the following argument: that the development of Ireland, North and South, over the past century and a half is explicable in terms of the development of social forces which found a coherent expression in nationalist ideology and ardent Catholicism and Orangeism.

These social forces have been fully and coherently integrated into an international production system in that period. The social and economic changes in the whole of Ireland since the sixties can then be related to effects on both States of the changed international circumstances since the Second World War. The institutions developed in the context of a previous international reality have proved inadequate to the changing circumstances and both States are severely dislocated socially, politically, economically and ideologically. This is not so in any modernization sense, but relates to the increasing power of social forces which the social institutions have proved unable to accommodate.

The initial seminars are geared towards an exposition of the bases of the present social institutions while the later seminars are directed towards an analysis of the destabilizing social forces.

The state recognises the Family as the natural primary and fundamental unit group of Society, and as a moral institution possessing inalienable and imprescriptable rights, antecedent and superior to all positive law.

The Irish Constitution
Article 41.1.1.

The National territory consists of the whole island of Ireland, its islands and territorial seas.

The Irish Constitution
Article 2

In olde tyme they much abused the honourable state of marriage, either in contractes vnlawfull, meetying the degrees of population, or in divorcementes at pleasure, or in retaynyng concubines or harlots for wyues: Yea even at this day where the clergy is fainte, they can be content to marry for a yeare and a day of probation, and at the yeres ende, or any tyme after, to returne hir home with hir marriage goodes or as much in valure, vpon light quarels, if the gentlewomans friendes be vnable to reuenge the iniury. In like maner may she forsake hir husband.

Raphael Holinshed
'Holinshed's Irish Chronicle'
(1577)

In Ireland there are two
acceptable reactions to a crisis.
The first is to get on your knees
and pray to God. The second is
to go down on one knee, lift a
gun, and try to shoot the head
off your opponent . . .

. . . But then remember; 'The
great are only great because we
are on our knees': Let us arise.

Rosita Sweetman
'On Our Knees'

In California we had proposition
13, seeking tax reform at the
expense of social services.
Maggie Thatcher came to power
on the same populist ticket. In
contrast, in Dublin last Spring we
had 250,000 trade unionists
demonstrating on the streets
demanding tax reform, but
based on the maintenance and
extension of social services.

Fergus Whelan
Vice-President, Dublin Trades Council

Photographs by Derek Speirs

I had 40,000 french letters in the station wagon and insisted they were all for my own personal use. I said I had imported them, I was going to use them, and if they booked me I would challenge them under EEC regulations. 'Ah, go away' they said finally.

Frank Crummey: Family Planning Services

Contraception is evil. It's the essence of evil.

Meena Cribbins: Mna na h-Eireann

Moral standards here, in my experience, are much the same as anywhere else. It's just being masked. The hypocritical surface conceals a very normal society.

Jim Fitzgerald

Quotes from 'On Our Backs' by Rosita Sweetman

Whereof the testimony given by Cambrensis, Spenser, Stanihurst, Hanmer, Camden, Barcly, Moryson, Davies, Campion and every other new foreigner who has written on Ireland from that time (the Norman invasion), may bear witness; inasmuch as it is almost according to the fashion of the beetle they act, when writing concerning the Irish. For it is the fashion of the beetle, when it lifts its head in the summer time, to go about fluttering, and not to stoop towards any delicate flower that may be in the field, or any blossom in the garden, although they may be all roses or lilies, but it keeps bustling about until it meets with dung of horse or cow, and proceeds to roll itself therein. . .

Geoffrey Keating
'History of Ireland'
written c. 1629

Martyn Turner Cartoon

Strabane, Northern Ireland
Brendan Gallagher and
Josephine Gallagher, father
and mother of Willie Gallagher,
hold two paintings painted by
their son in Long Kesh, 1977.
Willie was a 'political prisoner'
until that status was withdrawn
in 1977.

Since I cannot disguise from
myself the helpless dependence
of the British Empire on us for
vital elements of talent and
character (without us the English
race would simply die of respect-
ability within two generations),
I am quite ready to help the
saving work of reducing the sham
Ireland of romance to a heap of
unsightly ruins.

G B Shaw 1.2.1896

Acknowledgements

A Sense of Ireland is the result of a two year process, from conception to realisation. In that time hundreds of people have been involved in one way or another in helping to create the event. Each one is due thanks. As they are too numerous to mention only those whose contribution would otherwise pass unmentioned are listed as individuals, the rest in groups.

A Sense of Ireland exists thanks to the efforts of:

The multitude of Artists who have agreed to participate.
Seán MacRéamoinn Mary Mullin, and the Members of the Irish Organising Committee.
Philippa Kidd, Brigid Roden and the Staff of the Festival.
Terry O'Raffeartaigh and the Members of the Cultural Relations Committee.
David Andrews, John Lawton and the Staff of the Irish Department of Foreign Affairs.
The Directors and Staff of the Concerns which have sponsored this Festival.
The Irish Ambassador, the British Ambassador and the Embassy Staff in Dublin and London.
The Northern Ireland Office.
Ken Jamison and Colm O'Briain and the Members and Staff of the two Arts Councils in Ireland.
The Institutions and individuals who have contributed elements of the Festival.
Bill McAllister, Iwona Blaszcyk and all at the ICA.
The Directors and Staff of the host venues and visiting institutions.
Fintan Keogh, Chris Kane and all at Ireland House in London.
The Directors and Staff of the professional concerns which have serviced the Festival.
The Irish Societies, Clubs and Associations in London.

The Director's special thanks are due to those named above and to Eoin Dillon, Richard Eckersley, Mary Donohue, Brendan MacLua and Eoin Ryan.

Special thanks for their help on this catalogue are due to the following.
Books Upstairs, South King Street
Dolmen Press,
The Governors of Marsh's Library
The Irish Times
The National Library
The National Museum
The National Gallery
Turning-Point, South King Street

Thanks also to:
Charles and Carol Acton, Martin Armstrong, Derek Bailey, Millicent Bowerman, Russell Brown, Billy Boucher, John Behan, Jim Banbury, Mike Colgan, Sé Cleary, Caroline Crowther, Marcus Cleary, Lindy Dufferin, Leo Duffy, George Dawson, Lawrence Harbottle, Richard Garnet Harper, Marigold Johnson, Oisin Kelly, Monica Kinlay, Ron Mason, Ciarán MacMathúna, Tim Mara, John O'Callaghan, Myles O'Byrne, David O'Leary, Conall O'Sullivan, Liam and Maire de Paor, Tom Petzal, Luke Randolph, Norman Rosenthal, Tim Scott, Brendan Scannell, Michael Scott, Niall Stokes.

Quotations & Illustrations

We acknowledge permission to reprint the following extracts:

from *Murphy* by Samuel Beckett and *Langrishe Go Down* by Aidan Higgins, by kind permission of John Calder (Publishers) Limited;

from *The Pleasures of Gaelic Literature,* edited by John Jordan, Cork 1977, and from *Folk Music and Dances of Ireland* by Breandán Breathnach, Cork 1977, by permission of The Mercier Press;

from *Field Work and Door into the Dark* by Seamus Heaney, and from *The Battle of Aughrim* by Richard Murphy by permission of Faber and Faber Limited;

from *Drums under the Window* by Sean O'Casey by permission of Macmillan, London and Basingstoke;

from *Owning Up* by George Melly by permission of Weidenfeld (Publishers) Limited.

from *On Our Backs and On Our Knees,* both by Rosita Sweetman, published by Pan Books Ltd. 1979;

from *Lives* by Derek Mahon, published by the Oxford University Press, 1972;

from *A Visit to Castletown House* and *A Farewell To English* by Michael Hartnett, by permission of Dolmen Press.

from *Heartbreak House* by G. B. Shaw by permission of the Society of Authors, on behalf of the Bernard Shaw estate.

from *Ulysses* by James Joyce, by permission of the Bodley Head.

from *The Rough Field* by John Montague, by permission of Dolmen Press.

Photographs from the following sources were used as listed:

Page 18	Walter Pfeiffer
24–25	Richard Haughton
28	Walter Pfeiffer
32	Mike Bunn
39	Derek Speirs (IFL/Report)
47	Chris Robinson, no.2
57–60	Courtesy of the National Gallery of Ireland
55	Leslie Stannage, no.1
62	Lawrence Collection, National Library
64	Derek Speirs (IFL/Report)
65	Courtesy of the National Museum
67	Dublin Opinion' 1932
68	Courtesy of the National Library, no.1
68	Courtesy of na Píobairí Uilleann, no. 2
69	Bord Fáilte
76	Derek Speirs (IFL/Report)
78	Derek Speirs (IFL/Report)
80	John Davies
81	Walter Pfeiffer
84	Tony Murray
85	Rod Tuach
86	Tony Murray
87	Rod Tuach
88–89	Tom Kennedy
90	Derek Speirs (IFL/Report)
99	Marsh's Library/Chris Robinson
102	Walter Pfeiffer
104	Tom Lawlor/Irish Times
105	Beth Ridgell
106	Derek Speirs (IFL/Report)
108	Eamonn O'Dwyer (IFL/Report)
109	Beth Ridgell
112	Bernard Farrell/Hot Press
114	Eamonn O'Dwyer/IFL/Hot Press
116	James Mahon/Hot Press
117–18	Hot Press
119	Patrick Brocklebank/Hot Press
120	Hugo McGuinness /Hot Press
121	Hot Press
122	Bernard Farrell/Hot Press
126–127	Eamonn O'Dwyer (IFL/Report)
131	Courtesy of the National Gallery of Ireland
136	Derek Speirs (IFL)
137	Collection, Ulster Museum, Belfast
139	Lawrence Collection, National Library
142	Fergus Bourke
144	Jas D O'Callaghan ARPS
150	Lawrence Collection, National Library
151–152	Fergus Bourke
155	John Cullen, no. 1
155	Cork Examiner, no. 2
162	National Film Archive/Stills Library, London, nos. 1, 3, 4
162	Denis Johnston, no. 5
163	George Morrison, nos. 1-2
163	Derek Speirs (IFL/Report), no.3
164	Denis Johnston, no. 1
164	National Film Archive/Stills Library, London, nos. 2, 3
166	National Film Archive/Stills Library, London.
170	Derek Speirs (IFL/Report)
171	Tony Murray
172–73	Derek Speirs (IFL/Report)
175–76	Derek Speirs (IFL/Report)
Cover	Walter Pfeiffer
	Original Woodcuts from Holinshed's Irish Chronicle (1577) by courtesy of Dolmen Press

Summary of Events

Theatre

A Life
by Hugh Leonard
Directed by Joe Dowling
presented by The Abbey
Theatre, Ireland's National
Theatre Company. This follow-
up to Leonard's recent
Broadway success, *Da,* was the
undisputed triumph of the
Dublin Theatre Festival 1979
Old Vic, 4 – 16 February
Sponsored by Kerrygold and
B+I Line

*The Playboy of the Western
World*
Acclaimed folk-ballet version of
Synge's famous play presented
by the Irish Ballet Company with
original live music by The
Chieftains, Ireland's leading
group of traditional musicians.
Sadlers Wells, 4 – 8 March
Sponsored by Waterford Crystal

The Risen People
by James Plunkett
Directed by Jim Sheridan,
Plunkett's stage version of his
novel, *Strumpet City,* as adapted
by the Project Arts Centre
Theatre Company, Ireland's
most exciting experimental
company. The play is a graphic
description of life in Dublin
during the great 1913 Lock Out.
ICA Theatre, 6 – 23 February

The Liberty Suit
by Peter Sheridan
Directed by Jim Sheridan
Another Project Arts Centre
production. This tells how a
convicted arsonist becomes a
hero among his fellow inmates
in an Irish borstal until he
realises that some prisoners are
more equal than others.
Royal Court Theatre
28 February – 15 March

The Keytag
by Mike McGrath
Directed by Roger Michell. This
first production of expatriate
playwright McGrath, set in a
clothes shop in a small market
town, explores the everyday
relations of an Irish/English
family with alarming results.
Royal Court Upstairs
7 February – 1 March

*The Man Who Boxed Like John
McCormack*
by Ian McPherson
Directed by Roland Jacquerello
Boxer Jack Doyle's credentials
are vetted by St Peter at the
Golden Gates. Presented by the
British based Irish Touring Co,

Green Fields and Far Away.
Lyric Studio Theatre
11 – 16 February

*Now You See Him,
Now You Don't*
by J P O'Neill
Directed by Jeremy Mason
Presented by North London's
own Irish Theatre & Folk Club
Sugawn Theatre
12 February – 13 March
(Tues, Wed, Thurs)

The State of Emergency

A programme of events relating
to aspects of Northern Ireland:
Action Space (Drill Hall)
12 February – 2 March

Bringing it all back home
a photographic examination of
the Falls and the Shankill by
Camerawork.
12 February – 1 March

People of No Property:
a performance band from
Belfast.
14 – 16 February

New Wave Nights
with a selection of bands.
15, 22, 29 February

The Patriot Game:
a film by Arthur McCaig
16 February

*The Position of Women in
Ireland* – Theatre by the Women
of Ireland group.
21 February

Echoes from the North:
art performance by Sonia Knox
23 February

Ireland: behind the wire
a film by the Berwick Street
Collective.
23 February

*1980's: Spit and Polish Girlie
Show* by the Camouflage Group.
Theatre and Music.
23 February

O'Wilde and his Mother a new
play by Siobhan Lennon
performed by the 'Women of
Ireland' group.
28 February – 1 March

Home Soldier Home
A film by Chris Reeves
1 March

Belfast Video
1 March

*Shell Shock Rock and Other
Films:* recent film on the new-
wave scene in the North, plus all
films previously shown, and

more, can be seen from 3 p.m.
2 March
Action Space (Drill Hall)
12 February – 2 March

Visual Arts Exhibitions

Without the Walls
Conceptual art installations by
nine young artists all of whom
have exhibited internationally:
Brian King, Noel Sheridan, Nigel
Rolfe, Alanna O'Kelly, John
Aiken, Felim Egan, James
Coleman, Michael O'Sullivan
and Ciaran Lennon
ICA Main Gallery
15 February – 16 March

'The Delighted Eye . . .
Modern Irish painting, print and
sculpture. A major Arts Councils
in Ireland touring exhibition
comprising leading artists who
exploit the more traditional Irish
images. They include Edward
Maguire, Barrie Cooke, Patrick
Collins, Arthur Armstrong, Sean
McSweeney, Colin Middleton,
Charles Brady, Maria
Simmonds-Gooding, Norah
McGuinness, T P Flanagan,
Nano Reid, Louis le Brocquy,
Camille Souter, Brian Bourke,
Tony O'Malley, Gordon Woods,
Basil Blackshaw, John Kelly,
Charles Cullen, Alice Hanratty,
Anthony O'Carroll, Oisin Kelly,
F E McWilliam, John Behan,
Edward Delaney, Pat Connor, Jill
Crowley, Aileen McKeogh, Mary
Farl-Powers, Patrick Hickey,
David Crone and Neil
Shawcross
52 Earlham Street Gallery,
5 February – 5 March
Sponsored by Bank of Ireland

The International Connection
Modern Irish painting, print and
sculpture – the metropolitan
influence. All of the artists
involved have assimilated into
their work different aspects of
international developments in
the arts of the 70's and many
have achieved considerable
reputations abroad. They
include John Aiken, Robert
Ballagh, Michael Coleman,
Michael Craig-Martin, Rita
Donagh, Felim Egan, Michael
Farrell, Martin Gale, Tim
Goulding, Erik Adriaan Van der
Grijn, Colin Harrison, Brian
Henderson, Jeremy Henderson,
Roy Johnston, Cecil King, Theo
McNab, Donnagh McKenna,
Anne Madden, Clifford Rainey,
Patrick Scott, William Scott,
Sean Scully, Deborah Brown,

Michael Bulfin, John Burke, Adrian Hall, Brian King, Michael Warren, Alexandra Wejchert
Round House Gallery
26 February – 23 March
Sponsored by P. J. Carroll & Co.

Portrait of the Artist:
Abbey Theatre 1904-1979
J M Synge, Sean O'Casey, W B Yeats . . . just some of the great literary figures associated with the Abbey Theatre from 1904-79, whose portraits are featured in this exhibition, alongside Joyce, Shaw and many others.
The Fine Art Society
18 February – 7 March

Contemporary Irish Art Society Works on Paper
Theo McNab, Robert Ballagh, Vivienne Roche and Charles Harper are among over fifteen artists, most of them in the younger avant-garde category, with works in the collection of the Society, whose purpose is the promotion and patronage of Irish contemporary art.
Angela Flowers Gallery
13 February – 1 March

Jack B Yeats
Drawings and watercolours by Ireland's major 20th century artist.
Theo Waddington
14 February – 15 March.

Patrick Scott – Paintings
New work by one of Ireland's best known abstract painters.
Annely Juda Fine Art
13 February – 1 March.

Roy Johnston – Recent Work
New 'structure' work by one of Ulster's leading artists.
S. East Gallery
7 February – 9 March
(Thurs – Sun).

General Exhibitions

West of West
An artist's view of early Irish monuments and sites, emphasising the visual and mystical impact of this ancient heritage, presented in photos, drawings and slides with commentaries by Peter Harbison and John Sharkey.
ICA New Gallery
8 February – 16 March.
Sponsored by Bord Na Móna: The Irish Peat Development Authority

. . .No Country for Old Men'
This exhibition, using

photographs, diagrams, music, cartoons and text, sets the social and economic context for the artistic events of the festival; it explores how Ireland, in the past two decades, has changed more dramatically than any other country in Europe.
Compiled by Brian Torode, Hilary Tovey and James Wickham, Dept. of Sociology, Trinity College, Dublin and designed by Raymond Kyne.
ICA Concourse
6 February – 16 March
Sponsored by Allied Irish Banks

The Evolution of Irish Architecture: Traditions and Directions
Photographs and drawings of building and architecture in Ireland, from ancient monuments to future trends.
Royal College of Art
12 February – 7 March

The Irish Joke
Irish cartoonists examine every aspect of contemporary events in their particular manner, including work by: Tom Mathews, Littleman, Martyn Turner, Robert Armstrong, Rowel Friers, Bad Taste Productions Inc., and others.
The Workshop
18 February – 8 March

The Vikings in Ireland
Part of the major British Museum exposition on the life-style, movements and fate of the Vikings.
British Museum
14 February – 20 July

Irish Palladian Houses
Photographic presentation of the great country houses of the Georgian Age. Compiled by the National Trust Archive and the Irish Georgian Society.
Royal College of Art
12 February – 7 March

Books – A Sense of Ireland
Exhibition of publications from Irish publishing houses, and of work in English and Irish by living writers.
National Book League
4 February – 23 February
Sponsored by The Irish Export Board

Photographic Exhibitions

Ireland's Eye
Three Irish photographers examine their surroundings. Tony Murray's style has been described as 'Cartier-Bresson

with a brogue', while Tom Kennedy has poignantly recorded a fast-vanishing urban life and landscape; Rod Tuach's humorous pictures are wide-ranging in subject.
Photographers' Gallery
7 February – 2 March

Aspects of Ireland
Colour landscape photography by Walter Pfeiffer, a young German who has been living in Ireland since the early 'sixties.
Pentax Gallery
6 – 29 February

Three Points of View
Irish landscape through the eyes (or lens) of an Englishman, a Southern Irishman and a Northern Irishman. John Davies' recurring theme is the continually changing water-air-landscape of the West coast. Richard Haughton specialises in dreamily beautiful colour prints, while Bill Kirk portrays some unusual and fleeting aspects of the landscape in black and white.
Swiss Cottage Library
12 February – 12 March
Presented by Camden Borough Arts and Entertainments

Crafts Exhibitions

Weaving—The Irish Inheritance.
The work and environment of six contemporary weavers contrasted with that of their predecessors. The weavers are: Leonora Fowler, Helena Ruth, Muriel Beckett, Cecilia Gleadowe Stephens, Alice Roden, Sallie O'Sullivan.
Organised by the Crafts Council of Ireland
30 January – 29 March

Irish Patchwork
Highly praised Kilkenny Design Workshops exhibition of patchwork quilts of the last two centuries. Nominated for European Exhibition of the Year Award.
Somerset House
8 February – 15 March.
Sponsored by the Insurance Corporation of Ireland Ltd. and Irish Shipping Ltd.

Irish Pipes and Piping
Collection of about twenty examples of Uilleann pipes mainly from The National Museum, Dublin as well as a workshop area where present-day pipe makers will display and explain their craft. This living art will be demonstrated in daily

sessions with leading pipers Seamus Ennis, Liam O Floinn, Paddy Keenan and Pat Mitchell, among others, culminating in a major piping concert on 27 February. Breandán Breathnach, recognised expert on Irish folk music, will also give a lecture on piping. The exhibition has the active assistance of Na Píobairí Uilleann, the Association of Uilleann Pipers.
Battersea Arts Centre
6 February – 1 March

Literature

Irish Writing To-day: Writers Reading
The Novelists, Playwrights and Poets participating represent the best living Irish writers today and are: John Banville, Eavan Boland, Ciaran Carson, Eiléan Ní Chuilleanáin, Michael Davitt, Seamus Deane, Paul Durcan, Peter Fallon, Michael Hartnett, Seamus Heaney, John Hewitt, Aidan Higgins, Pearse Hutchinson, Denis Johnston, Jennifer Johnston, Neil Jordan, Brendan Kennelly, Benedict Kiely, Thomas Kilroy, Mary Lavin, Michael Longley, Thomas McCarthy, Tomás MacSíomóin, Aidan Mathews, John Montague, John Morrow, Paul Muldoon, Richard Murphy, Thomas Murphy, Liam O'Flaherty, Desmond O'Grady, Liam O'Muirthile, Frank Ormsby, Cathal O Searcaigh, Seán O Tuama, Mícheál O Siadháil, Stewart Parker, Tom Paulin, James Plunkett, Peter Sheridan, James Simmons, Francis Stuart, William Trevor.
National Poetry Centre
Readings every Tues. & Thurs.
5 February – 6 March
Sponsored by Guinness

Writers at the Round House
A series of readings by Irish authors

Readings by Seamus Heaney
3 February

John Montague's *The Rough Field*
A dramatised reading with music
17 February

Irish Language Poets and Traditional Music
24 February

Richard Murphy's *The Battle of Aughrim*
A dramatised reading with music
2 March

Reading by Thomas Kinsella
9 March
Sponsored by Guinness

Lectures at the Round House

Dr Christopher Ricks on Seamus
Heaney
3 February

Richard Cave on John
Montague
17 February

Declan Kiberd and Daithí
O hOgáin on Modern Irish
Writing and Folklore
24 February

Augustine Martin on Richard
Murphy
2 March

Seamus Deane on Thomas
Kinsella
9 March

Sponsored by Guinness

Film

Irish Cinema
A season of Irish-made films
ranging from early fiction works
of the 1910's to the new wave
of independent films of the
seventies by directors such as
Bob Quinn, Joe Comerford,
Cathal Black, Tom McArdle,
Kieran Hickey and Thaddeus
O'Sullivan, and RTE Films by
such producers as Brian
MacLochlainn and Louis Lentin.
National Film Theatre
4 – 28 February.

The Outsider's View
Four week season of over thirty
films showing British and
American cinema's peculiar
representation of Ireland and
the Irish, included are films such
as *Ulysses, The Informer, Man
of Aran* and *Odd Man Out* and
other classics by directors such
as Ford, Ophuls, Lean, Curtiz
and Flaherty.
ICA Cinema
7 – 29 February.
Sponsored by B+I Line.

Seminars on Film
ICA Seminar Room

British media and Ireland,
9 February, all day

British Cinema and Ireland,
16 February, all day

John Ford's Irish Films, Irish
Film culture
1 March, all day

Traditional Music
Week 1
The Chieftains and support
Albert Hall, 5 February
Watford Town Hall
7 February
Fairfield Croydon
8 February

Stockton's Wing and support
Gaumont State, Kilburn
9 February

Week 1 Support drawn from:
Tony Linnane and Noel Hill,
John Kelly snr, John Kelly jnr,
Joe Ryan, John Rea, Séamus
Tansey, Len Graham, Mairéad
Ní Dhómhnaill, Mary Bergin
plus London-based musicians

Week 2
Stockton's Wing and support
Civic Hall, Wimbledon
13 February

De Danann and support
Camden Centre 14 February
Gaumont State Kilburn
15 February
Poplar Civic Theatre
16 February

Week 2 Support drawn from:
Nollaig and Miriam Ní
Chathasaigh, Máire Ní Ghráda,
Des Wilkinson, Gerry O'Connor,
Martin O'Connor and Colm
Murphy, Frank Harte, Philip
King, Sarah and Rita Keane,
Peter O'Loughlin and Paddy
Murphy, Jimmy Crowley.

Week 3
Christy Moore and friends
Camden Centre 19 February

Andy Irvine and friends
Watford Town Hall
20 February

Week 3 Support drawn from
The Kenny Brothers, Maeve
Donnelly, Jim McKillop, Gary
Hastings and Gerry O'Donnell,
Mary Black, Sean Corcoran,
Paul Brock, Denis Ryan and
Patsy Hanley, David Hammond
and Artie McGlynn.

Week 4
The Dubliners and support.
Wembley Conference Centre,
26 February

Camden Jamboree with Tony
McMahon and Peadar Mercier, .
Denis Doody and Donal
O'Connor, Paddy Keenan, Paddy
Glackin plus London based
musicians
Irish Centre, Camden
27 February

Planxty, De Danann
Seamus Ennis, and support
Albert Hall
28 February

Week 4 Support drawn from:
Tony McMahon and Peadar
Mercier, Paddy Keenan and
Paddy Glackin, Dolores Keane
and John Faulkner, Liam
Weldon

*London-based musicians
include:* Roger Sherlock, John
Bowe, Raymond Roland, Bobby
Casey, Finbar Dwyer, Tom Carty,
Mary Conroy and Brendan
Mulkere, Danny Meehan,
Darach O Cathain, Sean
Cannon, Siobhán O'Donnell,
Donal McGuire

Series managed by Derek Block
Promotions

Siamsa Tíre
The National Folk Theatre of
Ireland.
An Irish festival of music, song,
mime and dance.
Sponsored by the Irish
Chaplains
Wembley Conference Centre
3 March

The Irish Woman in Song
Micheál O Súilleabháin, Nóirín
Ní Riain and support
Battersea Arts Centre
21, 22, 23 February

Comhaltas Ceoltóirí Eireann
National Kilburn, 12 February

Traditional music sessions
Half Moon Theatre
17, 24 February
Sugawn Folk Kitchen
15 February – 15 March (Fri – Sun)

Jazz/Contemporary

The Noel Kelehan Quintet
The best of Irish jazz featuring
John Wadham on drums and
Keith Donald on saxophone
Ronnie Scott's Club
4 – 16 February

The Louis Stewart Quartet
Regarded by many as the
world's finest jazz guitarist,
Louis Stewart represents the
strength of contemporary Irish
jazz.
Ronnie Scott's Club
18 February – 1 March

Paul Brady
Having broken away from his
traditional background Paul
Brady now stands at the
forefront of contemporary music
in Ireland.
The Venue
14 February

Concerts

RTE Academica String Quartet:
Mariana Sirbu-Dancila, violin;
Ruxandra Colan, violin;
Constantin Zanidache, viola;
Mihai Dancila-Sirbu, cello.
Programme:
Frederick May: *String Quartet in
C minor.*
Schubert: *String Quartet No. 14
in D minor 'Death and the
Maiden'.*
Wigmore Hall, 6 February
Sponsored by
Aer Lingus/London Tara Hotel

RTE Singers
Conductor: Eric Sweeney
Veronica McSwiney, Piano
Programme:
Works by Vaughan Williams,
Musgrave, Field, Beethoven,
Buckley, Boydell, Prokofiev,
Schubert, Poulenc and Potter
Wigmore Hall, 10 February
Sponsored by R.T.E.

Music North
Irene Sandford, Soprano. Jack
Smith, Baritone. Barry Douglas,
Piano. Havelock Nelson,
Accompanist.
Programme:
Music by Schubert, Wolf,
Beethoven, Walton, Liszt,
Ferguson, Harty, Hughes, Parke
and Wood.
Wigmore Hall, 12 February
Sponsored by Aer
Lingus/London Tara Hotel

John O'Conor, Piano
Programme:
Beethoven: *Sonata in C minor
Op. 111*
James Wilson: *Thermagistris.*
John Field: *Three Nocturnes.*
Gerard Victory: *Verona
Preludes.*
Lennox Berkeley: *Six Preludes.*
Scriabin: *Sonata No. 4 in F
sharp Op. 30.*
Wigmore Hall, 17 February
Sponsored by Aer
Lingus/London Tara Hotel

Bernadette Greevy, Mezzo with
John O'Conor, Piano
Programme:
Handel: *Three arias.*
Schumann: *Frauenliebe und
Leben.*
Ravel: *Cinq Mélodies Populaires
Grecques.*
Seóirse Bodley: *A Girl.*
Wigmore Hall, 19 February
Sponsored by Aer
Lingus/London Tara Hotel

Music by Gerald Barry
Lontano Ensemble
Beth Griffith, soprano

Decolletage for soprano/actress
– for three clarinets, two violas,
two cellos and piano/
harpsichord.
⊖ for two pianos.
Things that gain by being
painted for soprano, speaker,
cello and piano
ICA Theatre, 24 February

Ulster Orchestra
Conductor: Bryden Thomson.
Sheila Armstrong, Soprano
Programme:
Beethoven *Egmont Overture*.
Berlioz: *Nuit d'été*.
Brahms: *Serenade in D*.
St John's, Smith Square
29 February
Sponsored by Irish Shipping
Ltd. and the Insurance
Corporation of Ireland Ltd.

*A musical evening with
Geraldine O'Grady: violin ; Frank
Patterson: tenor ; Eily O'Grady:
piano/Irish harp*
Programme:
Music by Purcell, Ferguson,
Handel, Haydn, Kinsella, Kelly,
Moore, Aitken, Moore, Larchet
and Goddard.
Wigmore Hall, 2 March
Sponsored by Aer
Lingus/London Tara Hotel

RTE Symphony Orchestra
Conductor: Colman Pearce
Bernadette Greevy, Mezzo
Programme:
Gerard Victory:
Olympic Festival Overture.
Mahler:
*Lieder eines fahrenden
Gesellen.*
Tchaikowsky:
Symphony No. 5
Royal Festival Hall
10 March.
The concert is part of the RTESO
1980 European Tour

New Irish Chamber Orchestra
Conductor: Kenneth
Montgomery.
Mícheál O'Rourke, piano
Aisling Drury Byrne, cello.
Programme:
Thomas Arne:
Symphony No. 1 in C major.
Mozart: *Piano concerto No. 9 in
E flat K 271.*
John Kinsella: *Music for Cello
and Chamber Orchestra.*
Mozart: *Symphony No. 40
K550.*
Queen Elizabeth Hall
11 March.

Sponsored by Aer
Lingus/London Tara Hotel

Seminars

The Future of a Different Past

A series of Seminars covering
some of the major issues
affecting Ireland today.

*The Social Foundations of Irish
Nationalism*
Speaker: Milo Rockett
13 February

*Irish Populism and the
Twentieth Century State*
Speaker: Joseph Lee
15 February

*The Post World War II Social
Democratic Settlement in
Ireland*
Speaker: Gerry Sullivan
20 February

*Northern Ireland and the
Modern British State*
Speaker: Henry Patterson
22 February

Northern Ireland Loyalism
Speaker: Bernard Cullen
27 February

*The Restructuring of the
Southern State and Economy*
Speaker: James Wickham
29 February

Church, State and Morality
Speaker: John A Murphy
5 March

*Media in Ireland: the production
of the popular image*
Speaker: Eoghan Harris
7 March

Resources for change: Women
Speaker: Moira Woods
12 March

*Resources for Change: The
Trade Union Movement*
Speaker: Oliver O'Donohue
14 March

Seminars on 15 March:

*The future of the European
Periphery _ The effect of
Industrialisation on Agrarian
Social Formations*

*The future of Britain in the World
Production System – from
Economics towards
Development Strategy*

*The emerging Economic Powers
and the re-organisation of the
World Socio-Economic order*

*Structural dilemmas of the
World Production System –
beyond Keynesianism to
structural Economics*

*Ireland from Nationalism to
National Strategies*

Calendar of Events

Sunday 3 February

*5.00 Round House
Lectures at the Round House
Dr Christopher Ricks on Seamus Heaney

*7.30 Round House
Writers at the Round House
Reading by Seamus Heaney, Seamus Deane, Eiléan Ní Chuilleanáin

Monday 4 February

*9.30 – 5.30
National Book League
Books – A Sense of Ireland

*10 – 5 Crafts Council Gallery
Weaving – The Irish Inheritance
(opening Wednesday 30th January)

Irish Cinema
*6.30 National Film Theatre 1
Christmas Morning
Return to Glenescaul
Lament for Art O'Leary

*8.25 National Film Theatre 1
Irish Cinema:
Willy Riley and the Colleen Bawn

*7.30 Old Vic
Opening night
A Life
by Hugh Leonard
presented by the Abbey Theatre

*10pm – 1.30am Ronnie Scott's
Noel Kelehan Quintet

Tuesday 5 February

9.30 – 5.30
National Book League
Books – A Sense of Ireland

10 – 5 Crafts Council Gallery
Weaving – the Irish Inheritance

*10 – 8 52 Earlham St Gallery
The Delighted Eye . . .
Modern Irish Painting, Print and Sculpture

Irish Cinema
*6.15 and 8.30
National Film Theatre 2
Emtigon
Withdrawal
Down the Corner

*7.30
The National Poetry Centre
Writers Reading
Readings by Seamus Heaney

*7.30 Albert Hall
Traditional Music
The Chieftains with Noel Hill and Tony Linnane, Mairéad Ní

Dhómhnaill, John Rea, Len Graham & Mary Bergin plus London Musicians Raymond Roland, Bobby Casey & Roger Sherlock. Introduced by Doireann Ní Bhriain

7.30 Old Vic
A Life: Abbey Theatre Co

10pm – 1.30am Ronnie Scott's Club
Noel Kelehan Quintet

Wednesday 6 February

9.30 – 5.30
National Book League
Books – A Sense of Ireland

10 – 6 52 Earlham St Gallery
The Delighted Eye . . .

*10 – 4 Pentax Gallery
Aspects of Ireland
Photography by Walter Pfeiffer

10 – 5 Crafts Council Gallery
Weaving – The Irish Inheritance

*12 – 8 ICA Concourse & Foyer
. . . No Country for Old Men

*12 – 10 Battersea Arts Centre
Irish Pipes and Piping

Irish Cinema
*6.15 and 8.30
National Film Theatre 2
From Time to Time
The Dawn

*7.30 Wigmore Hall
RTE Academica String Quartet

7.30 Old Vic
A Life: Abbey Theatre Co

*8.00 ICA Theatre
Opening night
The Risen People
by James Plunkett
presented by Project Theatre Co

10pm – 1.30am
Ronnie Scott's
Noel Kelehan Quintet

Thursday 7 February

9.30 – 5.30
National Book League
Books – A Sense of Ireland

10 – 4 Pentax Gallery
Aspects of Ireland

10 – 5 Crafts Council Gallery
Weaving – The Irish Inheritance

10 – 8 52 Earlham St Gallery
The Delighted Eye . . .

10 – 10 Battersea Arts Centre
Irish Pipes and Piping

*11 – 7 Photographers' Gallery
Ireland's Eye
Three Irish photographers examine their surroundings

12 – 8 ICA Concourse & Foyer
. . . No Country for Old Men

*2 – 7 S. East Gallery
Roy Johnston – Recent Work

The Outsider's View
5.00 ICA Cinema
Home Soldier Home
A Place called Ardoyne

6.45 ICA Cinema
A Sense of Loss

9.10 ICA Cinema
People of Ireland

Irish Cinema
6.15 and 8.30 National Film Theatre 2
Faithful Departed
A Childs Voice
Exposure

7.30 Old Vic
A Life: Abbey Theatre Co

*7.30 National Poetry Centre
Writers Reading
Readings by William Trevor, Brendan Kennelly, Michael Longley, John Morrow.

8.00 ICA Theatre
The Risen People: Project Co

*8.00 Royal Court Upstairs
The Keytag
by Mike McGrath

*8.00 Watford Town Hall
Traditional Music
The Chieftains with John Kelly Snr & Jnr, and Joe Ryan, Seamus Tansey, Len Graham plus London Musicians

10pm – 1.30am
Ronnie Scott's
Noel Kelehan Quintet

Friday 8 February

9.30 – 5.30
National Book League
Books – A Sense of Ireland

10 – 4 Pentax Gallery
Aspects of Ireland

10 – 5 Crafts Council Gallery
Weaving – The Irish Inheritance

10 – 6 52 Earlham St Gallery
The Delighted Eye . . .

*10 – 7 Somerset House
Irish Patchwork

11 – 7 Photographers' Gallery
Ireland's Eye

*12 – 8 ICA New Gallery
West of West
Ancient Monuments: Irish Sites

12 – 8 ICA Concourse & Foyer
. . . No Country for Old Men

12 – 10 Battersea Arts Centre
Irish Pipes and Piping

2 – 7 S. East Gallery
Roy Johnston – Recent Work

The Outsiders' View
5.00 ICA Cinema

Home Soldier Home
A Place called Ardoyne
6.45 ICA Cinema
A Sense of Loss

9.10 ICA Cinema
People of Ireland

7.30 Old Vic
A Life : Abbey Theatre Co

8.00 ICA Theatre
The Risen People : Project Co

8.00 Royal Court Upstairs
The Keytag

•8.00 Fairfield Hall, Croydon
Traditional Music
The Chieftains with John Rea,
Seamus Tansey and Mairéad Ní
Dhómhnaill plus London
Musicians

10pm – 1.30am
Ronnie Scott's
Noel Kelehan Quintet

Saturday 9 February
9.30 5.30
National Book League
Books – A Sense of Ireland

•10 – 12.30, 2.15 – 6
ICA Seminar Room
Seminars on Film
British Media and Ireland

10 – 5 Crafts Council Gallery
Weaving – The Irish Inheritance

10 – 6 52 Earlham St Gallery
The Delighted Eye . . .

10 – 7 Somerset House
Irish Patchwork

10 – 10 Battersea Arts Centre
Irish Pipes and Piping

11 – 7 Photographers' Gallery
Ireland's Eye

12 – 8 ICA Concourse & Foyer
. . . No Country for Old Men

12 – 8 ICA New Gallery
West of West

2– 7 S East Gallery
Roy Johnston – Recent Work

*The Outsiders' View
5.00 ICA Cinema
The Patriot Game

6.45 ICA Cinema
A Sense of Loss

9.10 ICA Cinema
People of Ireland

7.30 The Old Vic
A Life : Abbey Theatre Co

8.00 Royal Court Upstairs
The Keytag

8.00 ICA Theatre
The Risen People : Project Co

•8.00 Gaumont State, Kilburn
Traditional Music
Stockton's Wing with Noel Hill

& Tony Linnane, Mary Bergin,
Len Graham and Mairéad Ní
Dhómhnaill plus London
Musicians

10pm – 1.30am
Ronnie Scott's
Noel Kelehan Quintet

Sunday 10 February
12 – 6 Somerset House
Irish Patchwork

12 – 6 Photographers' Gallery
Ireland's Eye

12 – 8 ICA New Gallery
West of West

12 – 8 ICA Concourse & Foyer
. . . No Country for Old Men

2 – 6 52 Earlham St Gallery
The Delighted Eye . . .

2 – 7 S. East Gallery
Roy Johnston – Recent Work

The Outsiders' View
5.00 ICA Cinema
The Patriot Game

6.45 ICA Cinema
A Sense of Loss

9.10 ICA Cinema
Ireland Behind the Wire

Irish Cinema
•6.15 and 8.30
National Film Theatre 2
Cloch
Self Portrait with Red Car
Poitin

•7.30 Wigmore Hall
RTE Singers, Veronica
McSwiney

Monday 11 February
9.30 – 5.30
National Book League
Books – A Sense of Ireland

10 – 4 Pentax Gallery
Aspects of Ireland

10 – 5 Crafts Council Gallery
Weaving – The Irish Inheritance

10 – 6 Battersea Arts Centre
Irish Pipes and Piping

10 – 7 Somerset House
Irish Patchwork

7.30 The Old Vic
A Life : Abbey Theatre Co

•8.00 Lyric Studio Theatre
The Man Who Boxed like John
McCormack
presented by Green Fields and
Far Away Theatre Co

8.00 Royal Court Upstairs
The Keytag

10 – 1.30 Ronnie Scott's
Noel Kelehan Quintet

Tuesday 12 February
9.30 – 5.30
National Book League
Books – A Sense of Ireland

•9.30 – 8.00
Swiss Cottage Library
Three Points of View
Photographs of Ireland

10 – 4 Pentax Gallery
Aspects of Ireland

10 – 5 Crafts Council Gallery
Weaving – The Irish Inheritance

•10 – 5.30 Royal College of Art
The Evolution of Irish
Architecture

•10 – 5.30 Royal College of Art
Irish Palladian Houses

10 – 7 Somerset House
Irish Patchwork

10 – 8 52 Earlham St Gallery
The Delighted Eye . . .

10 – 10 Battersea Arts Centre
Irish Pipes and Piping

11 – 7 Photographers' Gallery
Ireland's Eye

•11 – 9 Action Space
The State of Emergency
Bringing It All Back Home
A Camerawork Exhibition

12 – 8 ICA Concourse & Foyer
. . . No Country for Old Men

12 – 8 ICA New Gallery
West of West

The Outsiders' View
•5.00 ICA Cinema
Coilin and Platonida

6.45 ICA Cinema
A Sense of Loss

9.10 ICA Cinema
Ireland Behind The Wire

•6.15 RIBA
50 Years of Irish Architecture
a lecture by Patrick Delaney

•7.30
The National Poetry Centre
Writers Reading
Reading by Liam O'Flaherty,
Mary Lavin, Francis Stuart and
Denis Johnston.

•7.30 Wigmore Hall
Music North
Irene Sandford, Jack Smith,
Barry Douglas & Havelock
Nelson

7.30 Old Vic
A Life : Abbey Theatre Co

8.00 ICA Theatre
The Risen People : Project Co

8.00 Lyric Studio Theatre
The Man Who Boxed like John
McCormack

8.00 Royal Court Upstairs
The Keytag

•8.00 Sugawn Theatre
Now You See Him,
Now You Don't
by J P O'Neill

•8.00 National Club, Kilburn
Comhaltas Ceoltoírí Eireann
Concert

10pm – 1.30am
Ronnie Scott's
Noel Kelehan Quintet

Wednesday 13 February
9.30 – 5.30
National Book League
Books – A Sense of Ireland

9.30 – 8.00
Swiss Cottage Library
Three Points of View

10 – 4 Pentax Gallery
Aspects of Ireland

10 – 5 Crafts Council Gallery
Weaving – The Irish Inheritance

10 – 5.30 Somerset House
Irish Patchwork

10 – 5.30 Royal College of Art
The Evolution of Irish
Architecture

10 – 5.30 Royal College of Art
Irish Palladian Houses

10 – 6 52 Earlham St Gallery
The Delighted Eye . . .

•10 – 6 Annely Juda Fine Art
Patrick Scott – Paintings
Paintings by one of Ireland's
leading abstract artists

10 – 7 Somerset House
Irish Patchwork

•10.30 – 5.00
Angela Flowers Gallery
Works on Paper
The Contemporary Irish Arts
Society's Collection

11 – 7 Photographers' Gallery
Ireland's Eye

11 – 9 Action Space
The State of Emergency
A Camerawork Exhibition

12 – 8 ICA Concourse & Foyer
. . . No Country for Old Men

12 – 8 ICA New Gallery
West of West

12 – 10 Battersea Arts Centre
Irish Pipes and Piping

The Outsider's View
5.00 ICA Cinema
Coilin and Platonida

6.45 ICA Cinema
A Sense of Loss

9.10 ICA Cinema
Ireland Behind the Wire

Irish Cinema
6.15 National Film Theatre 2
Jack of all Maids
Mise Eire

8.30 National Film Theatre 2
These Stones Remain
Saoirse

•7.30 ICA
The Future of a Different Past
a series of seminars
The Social Foundations of Irish
Nationalism

7.30 Old Vic
A Life : Abbey Theatre Co

•8.00 Civil Hall, Wimbledon
Traditional Music
Stockton's Wing with Martin
O'Connor & Colm Murphy,
Nollaig & Miriam Ní
Chathasaigh & Máire Ní Ghráda,
Jimmy Crowley, Peter
O'Loughlin & Paddy Murphy

8.00 ICA Theatre
The Risen People : Project Co

8.00 Lyric Studio Theatre
*The Man Who Boxed Like John
McCormack*

8.00 Sugawn Theatre
*Now You See Him, Now You
Don't*

8.00 Royal Court Upstairs
The Keytag

10pm – 1.30am Ronnie Scott's
Noel Kelehan Quintet

Thursday 14 February
9.30 – 5.30
National Book League
Books – A Sense of Ireland

9.30 – 8.00
Swiss Cottage Library
Three Points of View

10 – 4 Pentax Gallery
Aspects of Ireland

•10 – 5 British Museum
The Vikings in Ireland
Part of the British Museum's
major Viking exhibition

10 – 5 Crafts Council Gallery
Weaving – The Irish Inheritance

10 – 5.30 Royal College of Art
Irish Palladian Houses

10 – 5.30 Royal College of Art
*The Evolution of Irish
Architecture*

•10 – 5.30 Theo Waddington
Jack B Yeats
Drawings and watercolours by
Ireland's major 20th century
artist

10 – 6 Annely Juda Fine Arts
Patrick Scott – paintings

10 – 7 Somerset House
Irish Patchwork

10 – 8 52 Earlham St Gallery
The Delighted Eye . . .

10 – 10 Battersea Arts Centre
Irish Pipes and Piping

10.30 – 5
Angela Flowers Gallery
Works on Paper

11 – 7 Photographers' Gallery
Ireland's Eye

11 – 9 Action Space
The State of Emergency
A Camerawork exhibition

12 – 8 ICA New Gallery
West of West

12 – 8 ICA Concourse & Foyer
. . . No Country for Old Men

2 – 7 S. East Gallery
Roy Johnston – Recent Work

The Outsiders' View
•5.00 ICA Cinema
The Gentle Gunman

7.00 ICA Cinema
Odd Man Out

9.00 ICA Cinema
The Outsider

Irish Cinema
6.15 National Film Theatre 2
Jack of all Maids
Mise Eire

8.30 National Film Theatre 2
These Stones Remain
Saoirse?

•7 – 3 The Venue
Paul Brady in Concert

•7.30 National Poetry Centre
Writers Reading
Readings by Seán O Tuama,
Paul Durcan, Thomas McCarthy,
Michael Davitt & John
Montague

7.30 Old Vic
A Life : Abbey Theatre Co

•8.00 Camden Centre
Traditional Music
De Danann with Des Wilkinson
& Gerry O'Connor, Frank Harte,
Philip King, Martin O'Connor
and Colm Murphy

•8.00 Action Space
The State of Emergency
People of No Property
a performance band from
Belfast

8.00 Lyric Studio Theatre
*The Man Who Boxed like John
McCormack*

8.00 ICA Theatre
The Risen People : Project Co

8.00 Royal Court Upstairs
The Keytag

8.00 Sugawn Theatre
*Now You See Him,
Now You Don't*

10pm – 1.30am
Ronnie Scott's
Noel Kelehan Quintet

Friday 15 February
9.30 – 5.30
National Book League
Books – A Sense of Ireland

9.30 – 8 Swiss Cottage Library
Three Points of View

10 – 4 Pentax Gallery
Aspects of Ireland

10 – 5 British Museum
The Vikings in Ireland

10 – 5 Crafts Council Gallery
Weaving – The Irish Inheritance

10 – 5.30 Royal College of Art
Irish Palladian Houses

10 – 5.30 Royal College of Art
*The Evolution of Irish
Architecture*

10 – 5.30 Theo Waddington
Jack B Yeats

10 – 6 Annely Juda Fine Art
Patrick Scott – Paintings

10 – 6 52 Earlham St Gallery
The Delighted Eye . . .

10 – 7 Somerset House
Irish Patchwork

10.30 – 5
Angela Flowers Gallery
Works on Paper

11 – 7 Photographers' Gallery
Ireland's Eye

11 – 9 Action Space
The State of Emergency
A Camerawork Exhibition

12 – 8 ICA Concourse & Foyer
. . . No Country for Old Men

12 – 8 ICA New Gallery
West of West

•12 – 8 ICA Main Gallery
Without the Walls
Sculptural installations by nine
young conceptual artists

12 – 10 Battersea Arts Centre
Irish Pipes and Piping

2 – 7 S. East Gallery
Roy Johnston—Recent Work

The Outsiders' View
5.00 ICA Cinema
Captain Boycott

7.00 ICA Cinema
Hennessy

9.00 ICA Cinema
The Outsider

•6.00 ICA Main Gallery
Without the Walls
Performance by Noel Sheridan

•7.30 ICA
The Future of a Different Past

Irish Populism and the 20th
Century State

•7.30 Action Space
The State of Emergency
New Wave Night

•7.30 Gaumont State, Kilburn
Traditional Music
De Danann with Nollaig &
Miriam Ní Chathasaigh Máire Ní
Ghráda, Jimmy Crowley, Frank
Harte, Sarah and Rita Keane.

7.30 Old Vic
A Life : Abbey Theatre Co

8.00 ICA Theatre
The Risen People : Project Co

8.00 Royal Court Upstairs
The Keytag

8.00 Lyric Studio Theatre
*The Man Who Boxed like John
McCormack*

•9.00 Sugawn Folk Kitchen
Traditional Music Session

10 pm – 1.30 am
Ronnie Scott's
Noel Kelehan Quintet

Saturday 16 February
9.30 – 5 National Book League
Books – A Sense of Ireland

9.30 – 5 Swiss Cottage Library
Three Points of View

10 – 1 Theo Waddington
Jack B Yeats

10 – 1 Annely Juda Fine Art
Patrick Scott – Paintings

10 – 5 British Museum
The Vikings in Ireland

10 – 5 Crafts Council Gallery
Weaving – The Irish Inheritance

•10 – 12.30, 2.15 – 6
ICA Seminar Room
Seminars on Film
British Cinema and Ireland

10 – 7 Somerset House
Irish Patchwork

10 – 10 Battersea Arts Centre
Irish Pipes and Piping

10 – 6 52 Earlham St Gallery
The Delighted Eye . . .

10.30 – 12.30
Angela Flowers Gallery
Works on Paper

11 – 7 Photographers' Gallery
Ireland's Eye

11 – 9 Action Space
The State of Emergency
A Camerawork exhibition

12 – 8 ICA Concourse & Foyer
. . . No Country for Old Men

12 – 8 ICA Main Gallery
Without the Walls

12 – 8 ICA New Gallery
West of West

2 – 7 S. East Gallery
Roy Johnston – Recent Work

The Outsiders' View
5.30 ICA Cinema
Ryan's Daughter

9.00 ICA Cinema
The Outsider

7.30 Old Vic. Last Night
A Life: Abbey Theatre Co.

***8.00** Poplar Civic Theatre
Traditional Music
De Danann with Martin
O'Connor & Colm Murphy, Peter
O'Loughlan & Paddy Murphy,
Philip King and Brian Mullen

***8.00** Action Space
The State of Emergency
People of No Property

8.00 ICA Theatre
*The Risen People: Project
Theatre Co.*

8.00 Royal Court Upstairs
The Keytag

8.30 Lyric Studio Theatre
(ends)
*The Man Who Boxed like John
McCormack*

9.00 Sugawn Folk Kitchen
Traditional Music Session

***9.30** Action Space
The State of Emergency
The Patriot Game

10pm – 1.30am
Ronnie Scott's
Noel Kelehan Quintet

Sunday 17 February

10 – 6 Battersea Arts Centre
Irish Pipes and Piping

12 - 6 Somerset House
Irish Patchwork

12 – 6 Photographers' Gallery
Ireland's Eye

12 – 8 ICA Concourse & Foyer
. . . No Country for Old Men

12 – 8 ICA New Gallery
West of West

12 – 8 ICA Main Gallery
Without the Walls

2 – 6 52 Earlham St Gallery
The Delighted Eye

2 – 7 S. East Gallery
Roy Johnston – Recent Work

2.30 – 6 British Museum
The Vikings in Ireland

***5.00** The Round House
Lectures at the Round House
Richard Cave on John
Montague

***7.30** Round House
Writers at the Round House
Dramatised reading, with music,
of 'The Rough Field'
by John Montague

The Outsiders' View
***5.30** ICA Cinema
Ryan's Daughter

9.00 ICA Cinema
The Outsider

Irish Cinema
***6.15 and 8.30** National Film
Theatre 2
Conquest of Light
Fleá Cheoil
Rocky Road to Dublin

***7.30** Wigmore Hall
John O'Conor, piano

***8.00** Half Moon Theatre
Traditional Irish Music Session

9.00 Sugawn Folk Kitchen
Traditional Music Session

Monday 18 February

***9.30 – 5.30**
The Fine Art Society
Portrait of the Artist
Portraits of the great literary
figures associated with The
Abbey Theatre 1904-1979

9.30 – 5.30
National Book League
Books – A Sense of Ireland

9.30 – 8 Swiss Cottage Library
Three Points of View

10 – 4 Pentax Gallery
Aspects of Ireland

10 – 5 British Museum
The Vikings in Ireland

10 – 5 Crafts Council Gallery
Weaving – The Irish Inheritance

10 – 5.30 Royal College of Art
Irish Palladian Houses

10 – 5.30 Royal College of Art
*The Evolution of Irish
Architecture*

10 – 5.30 Theo Waddington
Jack B. Yeats

10 – 6 Battersea Arts Centre
Irish Pipes and Piping

10 – 6 Annely Juda Fine Art
Patrick Scott – Paintings

10 - 7 Somerset House
Irish Patchwork

10.30 – 5
Angela Flowers Gallery
Works on Paper

***10.30 – 5.30** The Workshop
The Irish Joke
A selection of the best Irish
cartoonists exhibit their latest
work

8.00 Royal Court Upstairs
The Keytag

***10pm – 1.30am**
Ronnie Scott's
Louis Stewart Quartet
Ireland's renowned jazz guitarist
and friends

Tuesday 19 February

9.30 – 5.30
The Fine Art Society
Portrait of the Artist

9.30 – 5.30
National Book League
Books – A Sense of Ireland

9.30 – 8 Swiss Cottage Library
Three Points of View

10 – 4 Pentax Gallery
Aspects of Ireland

10 – 5 Crafts Council Gallery
Weaving – the Irish Inheritance

10 – 5 British Museum
The Vikings in Ireland

10 – 5.30 Royal College of Art
Irish Palladian Houses

10 – 5.30 Royal College of Art
*The Evolution of Irish
Architecture*

10 – 5.30 Theo Waddington
Jack B. Yeats

10.30 – 5.30 The Workshop
The Irish Joke

10 – 6 Battersea Arts Centre
Irish Pipes and Piping

10 – 6 Annely Juda Fine Art
Patrick Scott – Paintings

10 - 7 Somerset House
Irish Patchwork

10 – 8 52 Earlham St Gallery
The Delighted Eye . . .

10.30 – 5
Angela Flowers Gallery
Works on Paper

11 – 7 Photographers' Gallery
Ireland's Eye

11 – 9 Action Space
The State of Emergency
A Camerawork exhibition

12 – 8 ICA Concourse & Foyer
. . . No Country for Old Men

12 – 8 ICA Main Gallery
Without the Walls

12 – 8 ICA New Gallery
West of West

**The Outsiders' View*
5.00 ICA Cinema
Ulysses

7.00 ICA Cinema
The Informer

9.00 ICA Cinema
The Outsider

Irish Cinema
***6.15 – 8.30** National Film
Theatre 2
Yeats Country
Wheels
Kinkisha

***7.30** National Poetry Centre
Writers Reading
Reading by Pearse Hutchinson,
Michael Hartnett, Tomás Mac
Síomóin, Micheál O Siadhail

***7.30** Wigmore Hall
*Bernadette Greevy and John
O'Conor*

***8.00** Camden Centre
Traditional Music
Christy Moore and friends with
Kenny Brothers, Fred Finn &
Peter Horan, Jim McKillop, Mary
Black and David Hammond

8.00 ICA Theatre
The Risen People: Project Co.

8.00 Royal Court Upstairs
The Keytag

8.00 Sugawn Theatre
*Now You See Him,
Now You Don't*

10pm – 1.30am
Ronnie Scott's
Louis Stewart Quartet

Wednesday 20 February

9.30 – 5.30
The Fine Art Society
Portrait of the Artist

9.30 – 5.30
National Book League
Books – A Sense of Ireland

9.30 – 8 Swiss Cottage Library
Three Points of View

10 – 4 Pentax Gallery
Aspects of Ireland

10 – 5 The British Museum
The Vikings of Ireland

10 – 5 Crafts Council Gallery
Weaving – The Irish Inheritance

10 – 5.30 Royal College of Art
Irish Palladian Houses

10 – 5.30 Royal College of Art
*The Evolution of Irish
Architecture*

10 – 5.30 Theo Waddington
Jack B. Yeats

10 – 6 52 Earlham St Gallery
The Delighted Eye . . .

10 – 6 Annely Jude Fine Art
Patrick Scott – Paintings

10 - 7 Somerset House
Irish Patchwork

10.30 – 5
Angela Flowers Gallery
Works on Paper

10.30 – 5.30 The Workshop
The Irish Joke

11 – 7 Photographers' Gallery
Ireland's Eye

10 – 9 Action Space
The State of Emergency
a Camerawork exhibition

12 – 8 ICA Concourse & Foyer
. . . No Country for Old Men

12 – 8 ICA Main Gallery
Without the Walls

12 – 8 ICA New Gallery
West of West

12 – 10 Battersea Arts Centre
Irish Pipes and Piping

The Outsiders' View
5.00 ICA Cinema
Ulysses

7.00 ICA Cinema
The Plough and the Stars

9.00 ICA Cinema
The Outsider

●**7.30** ICA
The Future of a Different Past
The Post World War II Social
Democratic Settlement in
Ireland

●**8.00** Watford Town Hall
Traditional Music
Andy Irvine & Friends with
Denis Ryan & Patsy Hanley,
Gary Hastings & Gerry
O'Donnell, Paul Brock & Maeve
Donnelly and Sean Corcoran

8.00 ICA Theatre
The Risen People : Project Co

8.00 Sugawn Theatre
Now You See Him,
Now You Don't

8.00 Royal Court Upstairs
The Keytag

10pm – 1.30am Ronnie Scott's
Louis Stewart Quartet

Thursday 21 February

9.30 – 5.30
The Fine Art Society
Portrait of the Artist

9.30 – 5.30
National Book League
Books – A Sense of Ireland

9.30 – 8 Swiss Cottage Library
Three Points of View

10 – 4 Pentax Gallery
Aspects of Ireland

10 – 5 British Museum
The Vikings in Ireland

10 – 5 Crafts Council Gallery
Weaving – The Irish Inheritance

10 – 5.30 Theo Waddington
Jack B. Yeats

10 – 5.30 Royal College of Art
Irish Palladian Houses

10 – 5.30 Royal College of Art
The Evolution of Irish
Architecture

10 – 6 Annely Juda Fine Art
Patrick Scott – Paintings

10 - 7 Somerset House
Irish Patchwork

10 – 8 52 Earlham St Gallery
The Delighted Eye . . .

10 – 10 Battersea Arts Centre
Irish Pipes and Piping

10.30 – 5
Angela Flowers Gallery
Works on Paper

10.30 – 5.30 The Workshop
The Irish Joke

11 - 7 Photographer's Gallery
Ireland's Eye

11 – 9 Action Space
The State of Emergency
A Camerawork exhibition

12 – 8 ICA Concourse & Foyer
. . . No Country for Old Men

12 – 8 ICA Main Gallery
Without the Walls

12 – 8 ICA New Gallery
West of West

2 – 7 S. East Gallery
Roy Johnston – Recent Work

The Outsiders' View
5.00 ICA Cinema
Finnegan's Wake

7.00 ICA Cinema
How Green was my Valley

9.00 ICA Cinema
Portrait of the Artist as a Young
Man

Irish Cinema
6.15 and 8.15 National Film
Theatre 2
Killer Swim
Young and Old
Shell Shock Rock

●**7.30** National Poetry Centre
Writers Reading
Reading by playwrights Thomas
Kilroy, Thomas Murphy, Stewart
Parker, Peter Sheridan.

8.00 ICA Theatre
The Risen People : Project Co.

●**8.00** Action Space
The State of Emergency
The position of women in
Ireland: theatre presented by
The Women of Ireland group

●**8.00** Battersea Arts Centre
Micheál O Suilleabháin & Noirín
Ní Riain plus support
The Irish Woman in Song

8.00 Sugawn Theatre
Now You See Him,
Now You Don't

8.00 Royal Court Upstairs
The Keytag

10pm – 1.30am
Ronnie Scott's
Louis Stewart Quartet

Friday 22 February

9.30 – 5.30
The Fine Art Society
Portrait of the Artist

9.30 – 5.30
National Book League
Books – A Sense of Ireland

9.30 – 8 Swiss Cottage Library
Three Points of View

10 – 4 Pentax Gallery
Aspects of Ireland

10 – 5 Crafts Council Gallery
Weaving – The Irish Inheritance

10 – 5 British Museum
The Vikings in Ireland

10 – 5.30 Royal College of Art
Irish Palladian Houses

10 – 5.30 Royal College of Art
The Evolution of Irish
Architecture

- 5.30 Theo Waddington
Jack B Yeats

10 - 7 Somerset House
Irish Patchwork

10 – 6 Annely Juda Fine Art
Patrick Scott – Paintings

10 – 6 52 Earlham St Gallery
The Delighted Eye . . .

10 - 7 Somerset House
Irish Patchwork

10.30 – 5
Angela Flowers Gallery
Works on Paper

10.30 – 5.30 The Workshop
The Irish Joke

11 – 7 Photographers' Gallery
Ireland's Eye

11 – 9 Action Space
The State of Emergency
a Camerawork Exhibition

12 – 8 ICA Concourse & Foyer
. . . No Country for Old Men

12 – 8 ICA Main Gallery
Without the Walls

12 – 8 ICA New Gallery
West of West

12 – 10 Battersea Arts Centre
Irish Pipes and Piping

2 – 7 S. East Gallery
Roy Johnston – Recent Work

The Outsiders' View
5.00 ICA Cinema
The Puritan

7.00 ICA Cinema
The Quiet Man

9.15 ICA Cinema
Portrait of the Artist as a Young
Man

●**7.30** ICA
The Future of a Different Past
Northern Ireland and the
Modern British State

●**7.30** Action Space
The State of Emergency
New Wave Nite

8.00 ICA Theatre
The Risen People : Project Co.

8.00 Royal Court Upstairs
The Keytag

●**8.00** Battersea Arts Centre
Micheál O Súilleabháin &
Nóirín Ní Riain plus support

●**9.00** Sugawn Folk Kitchen
Traditional Music Session

10pm – 1.30am
Ronnie Scott's
Louis Stewart Quartet

Saturday 23 February

9.30 - 5.30 National Book
League (ends)
Book – A Sense of Ireland

10.30 – 12.30 Angela Flowers
Gallery
Works on Paper

10 – 1 Theo Waddington
Jack B Yeats

10 – 1 Annely Juda Fine Art
Patrick Scott – Paintings

10 – 1 The Fine Art Society
Portrait of the Artist

10 – 5 Swiss Cottage Library
Three Points of View

10 – 5 Crafts Council Gallery
Weaving – The Irish Inheritance

10 – 5 British Museum
The Vikings in Ireland

10 – 6 52 Earlham Street
Gallery
The Delighted Eye . . .

10 - 7 Somerset House
Irish Patchwork

10 – 10 Battersea Arts Centre
Irish Pipes and Piping

11 – 12.30 The Workshop
The Irish Joke

11 – 9 Action Space
The State of Emergency
A Camerawork Exhibition

12 – 6 Photographers' Gallery
Ireland's Eye

12 – 8 ICA Concourse & Foyer
. . . No Country for Old Men

12 – 8 ICA Main Gallery
Without the Walls

12 – 8 ICA New Gallery
West of West

2 – 7 S. East Gallery
Roy Johnston – Recent Work

*3.00 Action Space
The State of Emergency
Echoes from the North:
Sonia Knox performance

*The Outsiders' View
4.30 ICA Cinema
Finian's Rainbow

7.00 ICA Cinema
The Long Gray Line

9.00 ICA Cinema
Portrait of the Artist as a Young Man

Irish Cinema
*6.15 – 8.30
National Film Theatre 2
Pint of Plain
Guests of the Nation
The Beneficiary

8.00 ICA Theatre
Last Night
The Risen People: Project Co

*8.00 Action Space
The State of Emergency
Camouflage Theatre and Music
presents '1980 Spit and Polish
Girlie Show'

8.00 Royal Court Upstairs
The Keytag

*8.00 Battersea Arts Centre
Mícheál O Súilleabháin,
Nóirín Ní Riain plus support

*9.00 Sugawn Kitchen
Traditional Music Session

*9.00 Action Space
The State of Emergency
Ireland: behind the wire
Film by Berwick St. Collective

10 – 1.30 Ronnie Scott's
Louis Stewart Quartet

Sunday 24 February

10 – 6 Battersea Arts Centre
Irish Pipes and Piping

12 - 6 Somerset House
Irish Patchwork

12 – 6 Photographers' Gallery
Ireland's Eye

12 – 8 ICA Concourse & Foyer
. . . No Country for Old Men

12 – 8 ICA Main Gallery
Without the Walls

12 – 8 ICA New Gallery
West of West

2 – 7 S. East Gallery
Roy Johnston

2 – 6 52 Earlham St Gallery
The Delighted Eye . . .

2.30 – 6 British Museum
The Vikings in Ireland

*The Outsiders' View
4.30 ICA Cinema
A Fistful of Dynamite

7.00 ICA Cinema
The Rising of the Moon

9.00 ICA Cinema
Portrait of the Artist as a Young Man

*5.00 Round House
Lectures at the Round House
Declan Kiberd and Daithí O
hOgáin on Modern Irish Writing
and Folklore

*7.30 Round House
Writers at the Round House
Irish Language Poetry and
Traditional Music – with poets
Liam O Muirthile, Cathal O
Searcaigh, Johnny Chóil
Mhaidhc.

Irish Cinema
*6.15 and 8.30
National Film Theatre 2
Croagh Patrick
On a Paving Stone Mounted

*7.30 ICA Theatre
Gerald Barry
New Music

8.00 Half Moon Theatre
Traditional Irish Music Session

9.00 Sugawn Folk Kitchen
Traditional Music Session

Monday 25 February

9.30 – 5.30
The Fine Art Society
Portrait of the Artist

9.30 – 8 Swiss Cottage Library
Three Points of View

10 – 4 Pentax Gallery
Aspects of Ireland

10 – 5 British Museum
The Vikings in Ireland

10 – 5 Crafts Council Gallery
Weaving – The Irish Inheritance

10 – 5.30 Royal College of Art
Irish Palladian Houses

10 – 5.30 Royal College of Art
The Evolution of Irish Architecture

10 – 5.30 Theo Waddington
Jack B Yeats

10.30 – 5
Angela Flowers Gallery
Works on Paper

10.30 – 5.30 The Workshop
The Irish Joke

10 – 6 Annely Juda Fine Art
Patrick Scott – Painting

10 – 6 Battersea Arts Centre
Irish Pipes and Piping

10 - 7 Somerset House
Irish Patchwork

8.00 Royal Court Upstairs
The Keytag

10 – 1.30 Ronnie Scott's
Louis Stewart Quartet

Tuesday 26 February

9.30 - 5.30
Fine Art Society
Portrait of the Artist

9.30 – 8 Swiss Cottage Library
Three Points of View

10 – 4 Pentax Gallery
Aspects of Ireland

10 – 5 Crafts Council Gallery
Weaving – The Irish Inheritance

10 – 5 British Museum
The Vikings in Ireland

10 – 5.30 Royal College of Art
Irish Palladian Houses

10 – 5.30 Royal College of Art
The Evolution of Irish Architecture

10 – 5.30 Theo Waddington
Jack B Yeats

10 – 6 Annely Juda Fine Art
Patrick Scott – Paintings

10 – 6 Battersea Arts Centre
Irish Pipes and Piping

10 - 7 Somerset House
Irish Patchwork

10 – 8 52 Earlham St Gallery
The Delighted Eye . . .

10.30 – 5
Angela Flowers Gallery
Works on Paper

10.30 – 5.30 The Workshop
The Irish Joke

11– 7 Photographers' Gallery
Ireland's Eye

11 – 9 Action Space
The State of Emergency
A Camerawork Exhibition

*12 – 5.30
Round House Gallery
The International Connection
Irish Art of the 70's

12 – 8 ICA Main Gallery
Without the Walls

12 – 8 ICA New Gallery
West of West

12– 8 ICA Concourse & Foyer
. . . No Country for Old Men

*The Outsiders' View
5.00 ICA Cinema
Angels with Dirty Faces

7.00 ICA Cinema
The Last Hurrah

9.00 ICA Cinema
Portrait of the Artist as a Young Man

*Irish Cinema
*6.00 and **8.30** National Film
Theatre 2
A Week in the Life of Martin Cluxton
Deeply Regretted By . . .

*7.30 National Poetry Centre
Writers Reading
Reading by John Hewitt, Ciaran
Carson, Tom Paulin, Aidan
Mathews

8.00 Sugawn Theatre
Now You See Him, Now You Don't

8.00 Royal Court Upstairs
The Keytag

*8.00 Wembley Conference
Centre
The Dubliners with Tony
McMahon and Peadar Mercier,
Paddy Keenan, Paddy Glackin,
Dolores Keane and John
Faulkner, Liam Weldon

10pm – 1.30am
Ronnie Scott's
Louis Stewart Quartet

Wednesday 27 February

9.30 – 5.30
The Fine Art Society
Portrait of the Artist

9.30 – 8 Swiss Cottage Library
Three Points of View

10 – 4 Pentax Gallery
Aspects of Ireland

10 – 5 Crafts Council Gallery
Weaving – The Irish Inheritance

10 – 5 British Museum
The Vikings in Ireland

10 – 5.30 Theo Waddington
Jack B Yeats

10 – 5.30 Royal College of Art
The Evolution of Irish Architecture

10 – 5.30 Royal College of Art
Irish Palladian Houses

10 – 6 Annely Juda Fine Art
Patrick Scott – paintings

10 – 6 52 Earlham Street
Gallery
The Delighted Eye . . .

10 - 7 Somerset House
Irish Patchwork

10.30 – 5 Angela Flowers
Gallery
Works on Paper

10.30 – 5.30 The Workshop
The Irish Joke

11– 7 Photographers' Gallery
Ireland's Eye

11 – 9 Action Space
The State of Emergency
A Camerawork Exhibition

12 – 5.30
Round House Gallery
The International Connection

12 – 8 ICA Concourse & Foyer
. . . No Country for Old Men

12 – 8 ICA Main Gallery
Without the Walls

12 – 8 ICA New Gallery
West of West

12 – 10 Battersea Arts Centre
Irish Pipes and Piping

*The Outsiders' View
5.00 ICA Cinema
Man of Aran
Rory O'More

7.00 ICA Cinema
Donovan's Reef

9.00 ICA Cinema
Portrait of the Artist as a Young
Man

*7.30 ICA
The Future of a Different Past
Northern Ireland Loyalism

*8.00 Irish Centre, Camden
Camden Jamboree with Tony
McMahon and Peader Mercier,
Denis Doody and Donal
O'Connor, Paddy Glackin, Paddy
Keenan, Dolores Keane and
John Faulkner, Liam Weldon
plus London Musicians.

8.00 Sugawn Theatre
*Now You See Him, Now You
Don't*

8.00 Royal Court Upstairs
The Keytag

*8.00 Battersea Arts Centre
Piping Concert featuring
Seamus Ennis, Paddy Keenan,
Liam O Floinn and others

10pm – 1.30am
Ronnie Scott's
Louis Stewart Quartet

Thursday 28 February

9.30 – 5.30 The Fine Art
Society
Portrait of the Artist

9.30 – 8 Swiss Cottage Library
Three Points of View

10 – 4 Pentax Gallery
Aspects of Ireland

10 – 5 Crafts Council Gallery
Weaving – The Irish Inheritance

10 – 5 British Museum
The Vikings in Ireland

10 – 5.30 Theo Waddington
Jack B Yeats

10 – 5.30 Royal College of Art
*The Evolution of Irish
Architecture*

10 – 5.30 Royal College of Art
Irish Palladian Houses

10 – 6 Annely Juda Fine Art
Patrick Scott – Paintings

10 – 7 Somerset House
Irish Patchwork

10 – 8 52 Earlham St Gallery
The Delighted Eye . . .

10 – 10 Battersea Arts Centre
Irish Pipes and Piping

10.30 – 5
Angela Flowers Gallery
Works on Paper

10.30 – 5.30 The Workshop
The Irish Joke

11 – 7 Photographers' Gallery
Ireland's Eye

11 – 9 Action Space
State of Emergency
Camerawork Exhibition

12 – 5.30
Round House Gallery
The International Connection

12 – 8 ICA Main Gallery
Without the Walls

12 – 8 ICA New Gallery
West of West

12 – 8 ICA Concourse & Foyer
No Country for Old Men

2 – 7 S East Gallery
Roy Johnston – recent work

*Irish Cinema
5.30 ICA Cinema
*On a Paving Stone Mounted
Down the Corner*

**Irish Cinema
(ends)*
6.15 National Film Theatre 2
It's a Hard Oul' Station
Will to Win
Terminus: Gola Island

8.30 National Film Theatre 2
Down There
Three Funerals
Shankill Road

*7.30 National Poetry Centre
Irish Writing Today
Reading by Benedict Kiely, Neil
Jordan, Paul Muldoon, Peter
Fallon

*7.45 Albert Hall
Planxty, Seamus Ennis, De
Danann Tony McMahon and
Peadar Mercier, Paddy Keenan
and Paddy Glackin plus London
Musicians
Introduced by Dolly McMahon

*8.00 Royal Court Theatre
(opening night)
The Liberty Suit: Project Co.

8.00 Royal Court Upstairs
The Keytag

8.00 Sugawn Theatre
*Now you see him,
Now you don't*

*8.00 Action Space
The State of Emergency
O'Wilde and his mother

10pm – 1.30am
Ronnie Scott's
Louis Stewart Quartet

Friday 29 February

9.30 – 5.30
The Fine Art Society
Portrait of the Artist

9.30 – 8 Swiss Cottage Library
Three Points of View

10 – 4 Pentax Gallery (ends)
Aspects of Ireland

10 – 5 British Museum
The Vikings in Ireland

10 – 5 Crafts Council Gallery
Weaving – The Irish Inheritance

10 – 5.30 Theo Waddington
Jack B Yeats

10 – 5.30 Royal College of Art
*The Evolution of Irish
Architecture*

10 – 5.30 Royal College of Art
Irish Palladian Houses

10 – 6 52 Earlham St Gallery
The Delighted Eye . . .

10 – 6 Annely Juda Fine Art
Patrick Scott – Paintings

10 - 7 Somerset House
Irish Patchwork

10.30 – 5
Angela Flowers Gallery
Works on Paper

10.30 – 5.30 The Workshop
The Irish Joke

11 - 7 Photographer's Gallery
Ireland's Eye

11 – 9 Action Space
The State of Emergency
Camerawork Exhibition

12 – 5.30 Round House
The International Connection

12 – 8 ICA Main Gallery
Without the Walls

12 – 8 ICA New Gallery
West of West

12 – 8 ICA Concourse & Foyer
. . . No Country for Old Men

12 – 10 Battersea Arts Council
Irish Pipes and Piping

2 – 7 S. East Gallery
Roy Johnston – recent work

*5.30 *Irish Cinema*
ICA Cinema
On a Paving Stone Mounted
Down the Corner

*7.30 ICA
The Future of a Different Past
The Re-structuring of the
Southern State and Economy

*7.30 St John's Smith Square
The Ulster Orchestra

8.00 Royal Court Theatre
The Liberty Suit: Project Co.

8.00 Royal Court Upstairs
The Keytag

*8.00 Action Space
The State of Emergency
New Wave Night

9.00 Sugawn Folk Kitchen
Traditional Music Session

10pm – 1.30am
Ronnie Scott's
Louis Stewart Quartet

Saturday 1 March

9.30 – 5 Swiss Cottage Library
Three Points of View

*Seminars on Film
ICA Seminar Room
10 – 12.30 John Ford's Irish
films
2.15 Irish Film culture

10 – 1 Theo Waddington
Jack B Yeats

10 – 1 The Fine Art Gallery
Portrait of the Artist

10 – 1 Annely Juda Fine Art
(ends)
Patrick Scott – Paintings

10 – 5 British Museum
The Vikings in Ireland

10 – 5 Crafts Council Gallery
Weaving – The Irish Inheritance

10 – 6 52 Earlham St Gallery
The Delighted Eye . . .

10 - 7 Somerset House
Irish Patchwork

10 – 10 Battersea Arts Centre
(ends)
Irish Pipes and piping

10.30 – 12.30
Angela Flowers Gallery (ends)
Works on Paper

11 – 12.30 The Workshop
The Irish Joke

11 – 7 Photographers' Gallery
Ireland's Eye

11 – 9 Action Space
The State of Emergency
Camerawork exhibition (ends)

12 – 5.30
Round House Gallery
The International Connection

12 – 8 ICA New Gallery
West of West

12 – 8 ICA Concourse & Foyer
. . . No Country for Old Men

12 – 8 ICA Main Gallery
Without the Walls

2 – 7 S. East Gallery
Roy Johnston – Recent works

8.00 Action Space
The State of Emergency

O'Wilde and his mother (ends)

8.00 Royal Court Upstairs
The Keytag (ends)

8.00 Royal Court Theatre
The Liberty Suit: Project Co

9.00 Sugawn Folk Kitchen
Traditional Music Session

*9.30 Action Space
The State of Emergency
Home Solder Home. A film by Chris Reeves

10pm – 1.30am
Ronnie Scott's
Louis Stewart Quartet

Sunday 2 March

12 - 6 Somerset House
Irish Patchwork

12 – 6 Photographer's Gallery
(ends) *Ireland's Eye*

12 – 8 ICA Concourse & Foyer
. . . No Country for Old Men

12 – 8 ICA Main Gallery
Without the Walls

12 – 8 ICA New Gallery
West of West

2 – 6 52 Earlham St Gallery
The Delighted Eye . . .

2 – 7 S East Gallery
Roy Johnston – recent work

2.30 – 6 British Museum
The Vikings in Ireland

*3.00 Action Space
The State of Emergency
Shell Shock Rock plus
re-showing of all films and
others besides

*5.00 Round House
Lectures in the Round House
Augustine Martin on Richard
Murphy

*7.30 Round House
Writers at the Round House
Dramatised reading, with music,
of 'The Battle of Aughrim' by
Richard Murphy

*7.30 Wigmore Hall
*Musical evening with Geraldine
O'Grady, Frank Patterson and
Eily O'Grady*

9.00 Sugawn Folk Kitchen
Traditional Music Session

Monday 3 March

9.30 – 5.30 Fine Art Society
Portrait of the Artist

9.30 – 8 Swiss Cottage Library
Three Points of View

10 – 5 Crafts Council Gallery
Weaving – The Irish Inheritance

10 – 5 British Museum
The Vikings in Ireland

10 – 5.30 Theo Waddington
Jack B Yeats

10 – 5.30 Royal College of Art
*The Evolution of Irish
Architecture*

10 – 5.30 Royal College of Art
Irish Palladian Houses

10 - 7 Somerset House
Irish Patchwork

10.30 – 5.30 The Workshop
The Irish Joke

12 – 5.30
Round House Gallery
The International Connection

8.00 Royal Court Theatre
The Liberty Suit: Project Co

*8 – 10
Wembley Conference Centre
*Siamsa Tíre – a festival of
music, song, mime and dance.*

Tuesday 4 March

9.30 – 5.30
Fine Art Society
Portrait of the Artist

9.30 – 8 Swiss Cottage Library
Three Points of View

10 – 5 Crafts Council Gallery
Weaving – The Irish Inheritance

10 – 5 British Museum
The Vikings in Ireland

10 – 5.30 Theo Waddington
Jack B Yeats

10 – 5.30 Royal College of Art
*The Evolution of Irish
Architecture*

10 – 5.30 Royal College of Art
Irish Palladian Houses

10 - 5.30 The Workshop
The Irish Joke

10 – 5.30 Somerset House
Irish Patchwork

10 - 8 52 Earlham St Gallery
The Delighted Eye . . .

12 – 5.30
Round House Gallery
The International Connection

12 – 8 ICA Concourse & Foyer
. . . No Country for Old Men

12 – 8 ICA Main Gallery
Without the Walls

12 – 8 ICA New Gallery
West of West

*7.30 National Poetry Society
Writers Reading
Reading by James Plunkett,
Eavan Boland, Jennifer

Johnston, Frank Ormsby,
Richard Murphy

*7.30 Sadlers Wells
Opening Night
Playboy of the Western World
A folk ballet of Synge's play by
the Irish Ballet Company with
music by The Chieftains

8.00 Royal Court Theatre
The Liberty Suit: Project Co

8.00 Sugawn Theatre
Now you see him Now you don't

Wednesday 5 March

9.30 – 5.30
Fine Art Society
Portrait of the Artist

9.30 – 8 Swiss Cottage Library
Three Points of View

10 – 5 British Museum
The Vikings in Ireland

10 – 5 Crafts Council Gallery
Weaving – The Irish Inheritance

10 – 5.30 Royal College of Art
*The Evolution of Irish
Architecture*

10 – 5.30 Royal College of Art
Irish Palladian Houses

10.30 – 5.30 The Workshop
The Irish Joke

10 – 5.30 Theo Waddington
Jack B Yeats

10 – 6 52 Earlham Street
Gallery (ends)
The Delighted Eye . . .

10 - 7 Somerset House
Irish Patchwork

12 – 5.30
Round House Gallery
The International Connection

12 – 8 ICA Concourse & Foyer
. . . No Country for Old Men

12 – 8 ICA Main Gallery
Without the Walls

12 – 8 ICA New Gallery
West of West

7.30 ICA
The Future of a Different Past
Church, State and Morality

7.30 Sadlers Wells
*The Playboy of the Western
World*

8.00 Royal Court Theatre
The Liberty Suit: Project Co.

8.00 Sugawn Theatre
Now you see him Now you don't

Thursday 6 March

9.30 – 5.30 Fine Art Society
Portrait of the Artist

9.30 – 8 Swiss Cottage Library
Three Points of View

10 – 5 Crafts Council Gallery
Weaving – The Irish Inheritance

10 – 5 British Museum
The Vikings in Ireland

10 – 5.30 Theo Waddington
Jack B Yeats

10 – 5.30 Royal College of Art
*The Evolution of Irish
Architecture*

10 – 5.30 Royal College of Art
Irish Palladian Houses

10.30 – 5.30 The Workshop
The Irish Joke

12 – 5.30
Round House Gallery
The International Connection

10 - 7 Somerset House
Irish Patchwork

12 – 8 ICA Concourse & Foyer
. . . No Country for Old Men

12 – 8 ICA Main Gallery
Without the Walls

12 – 8 ICA New Gallery
West of West

2 – 7 S. East Gallery
Roy Johnston – recent work

*7.30 National Poetry Centre
Irish Writing Today
Reading by Aidan Higgins, John
Banville, Desmond O'Grady,
James Simmons

7.30 Sadlers Wells
*The Playboy of the Western
World*

8.00 Royal Court Theatre
The Liberty Suit: Project Co.

8.00 Sugawn Theatre
Now you see him, Now you don't

Friday 7 March

9.30 – 5.30 The Fine Art
Society
(ends) *Portrait of the Artist*

9.30 – 8 Swiss Cottage Library
Three Points of View

10 – 5 Crafts Council Gallery
Weaving – The Irish Inheritance

10 – 5 British Museum
The Vikings in Ireland

10 – 5.30 Theo Waddington
Jack B Yeats

10 – 5.30 Royal College of Art
*The Evolution of Irish
Architecture* (ends)

10 – 5.30 Royal College of Art
(ends)
Irish Palladian Houses

10 – 7 Somerset House
Irish Patchwork

10.30 – 5.30 The Workshop
The Irish Joke

12 – 5.30
Round House Gallery
The International Connection

12 – 8 ICA Main Gallery
Without the Walls

12 – 8 ICA New Gallery
West of West

12 – 8 ICA Concourse & Foyer
. . .No Country for Old Men

2 – 7 S. East Gallery
Roy Johnston – recent work

*2 - 5 Members' Room, Nash House
Joint Seminar on Design
featuring the Society of Industrial Artists and Designers and the Society of Designers in Ireland.

*7.30 ICA
The Future of a Different Past
Media in Ireland, the Production of the Popular Image.

8.00 Sadlers Wells
The Playboy of the Western World

8.00 Royal Court Theatre
The Liberty Suit: Project Co

9.00 Sugawn Folk Kitchen
Traditional Music Session

Saturday 8 March

9.30 – 5 Swiss Cottage Library
Three Points of View

10 – 1 Theo Waddington
Jack B Yeats

10 – 5 Crafts Council Gallery
Weaving – The Irish Inheritance

10 – 5 British Museum
The Vikings in Ireland

10 – 7 Somerset House
Irish Patchwork

10.30 – 5.30 The Workshop
The Irish Joke

12 – 5.30
Round House Gallery
The International Connection

12 – 8 ICA Concourse & Foyer
. . . No Country for Old Men

12 – 8 ICA Main Gallery
Without the Walls

12 – 8 ICA New Gallery
West of West

2 – 7 S. East Gallery
Roy Johnston – recent work

2.30 & 8.00 Sadlers Wells
The Playboy of the Western World (ends)

8.00 The Royal Court Theatre
The Liberty Suit: Project Co.

9.00 Sugawn Folk Kitchen
Traditional Music Session

Sunday 9 March

12 - 6 Somerset House
Irish Patchwork

12 – 8 ICA Main Gallery
Without the Walls

12 – 8 ICA New Gallery
West of West

12 – 8 ICA Concourse & Foyer
. . . No Country for Old Men

2 – 7 S. East Gallery (ends)
Roy Johnston – recent work

2.30 – 6 British Museum
The Vikings in Ireland

*5.00 Round House
Lectures in the Round House
Lecture by Seamus Deane on Thomas Kinsella

*7.30 Round House
Writers at the Round House
Readings by Thomas Kinsella

9.00 Sugawn Folk Kitchen
Traditional Music Session

Monday 10 March

9.30 – 8 Swiss Cottage Library
Three Points of View

10 – 5 Crafts Council Gallery
Weaving – The Irish Inheritance

10 – 5 British Museum
The Vikings in Ireland

10 – 5.30 Theo Waddington
Jack B Yeats

10 – 7 Somerset House
Irish Patchwork

12 – 5.30
Round House Gallery
The International Connection

*7.30 Royal Festival Hall
RTE Symphony Orchestra with Bernadette Greevy, Mezzo
Conductor: Colman Pearce
Part of major European Tour

8.00 Royal Court Theatre
The Liberty Suit: Project Co

Tuesday 11 March

9.30 – 8 Swiss Cottage Library
Three Points of View

10 – 5 Crafts Council Gallery
Weaving – The Irish Inheritance

10 – 5 British Museum
The Vikings in Ireland

10 - 5.30 Theo Waddington
Jack B Yeats

10 – 5.30 Somerset House
Irish Patchwork

12 – 5.30
Round House Gallery
The International Connection

12 – 8 ICA Concourse & Foyer
. . . No Country for Old Men

12 – 8 ICA Main Gallery
Without the Walls

12 – 8 ICA New Gallery
West of West

7.45 Queen Elizabeth Hall
New Irish Chamber Orchestra
with Mícheál O'Rourke, piano and Aisling Drury Byrne, cello
Conductor: Kenneth Montgomery

8.00 Royal Court Theatre
The Liberty Suit: Project Co

8.00 Sugawn Theatre
Now you see him, Now you don't

Wednesday 12 March

9.30 – 8 Swiss Cottage Library

10 – 5 Crafts Council Gallery
Weaving – The Irish Inheritance

10 – 5 British Museum
The Vikings in Ireland

10 – 5.30 Theo Waddington
Jack B Yeats

10 – 7 Somerset House
Irish Patchwork

12 – 5.30
Round House Gallery
The International Connection

12 – 8 ICA Concourse & Foyer
. . . No Country for Old Men

12 – 8 ICA Main Gallery
Without the Walls

12 – 8 ICA New Gallery
West of West

*7.30 ICA
The Future of a Different Past
Resources for Change: Women

8.00 Royal Court Theatre
The Liberty Suit: Project Co.

8.00 Sugawn Theatre
Now you see him, Now you don't

Thursday 13 March

10 – 5 Crafts Council Gallery
Weaving – The Irish Inheritance

10 – 5 British Museum
Vikings in Ireland

10 – 5.30 Theo Waddington
Jack B Yeats

10 – 7 Somerset House
Irish Patchwork

12 – 5.30 Round House Gallery
The International Connection

12 – 8 ICA Concourse & Foyer
. . . No Country for Old Men

12 – 8 ICA Main Gallery
Without the Walls

12 – 8 ICA New Gallery
West of West

8.00 Royal Court Theatre
The Liberty Suit: Project Co

8.00 Sugawn Theatre
Now you see him, Now you don't
(ends)

Friday 14 March

10 – 5 Crafts Council Gallery
Weaving – The Irish Inheritance

10 – 5 British Museum
The Vikings in Ireland

10 – 5.30 Theo Waddington
Jack B Yeats

10 – 7 Somerset House
Irish Patchwork

12 – 5.30 Round House
The International Connection

12 – 8 ICA Concourse & Foyer
. . . No Country for Old Men

12 – 8 ICA Main Gallery
Without the Walls

12 – 8 ICA New Gallery
West of West

*7.30 ICA
The Future of a Different Past
Resources for Change: The Trade Union Movement

8.00 Royal Court Theatre
The Liberty Suit: Project Co

9.00 Sugawn Folk Kitchen
Traditional Music Session

Saturday 15 March

10 – 1 Theo Waddington
(ends) *Jack B Yeats*

10 – 5 Crafts Council Gallery
(until 29 March)
Weaving – The Irish Inheritance

10 – 5 British Museum
(ends 20 July)
The Vikings in Ireland

10 - 5 Seminar Room, ICA
The Future of a Different Past
5 papers

10 – 7 Somerset House
(ends) *Irish Patchwork*

12 – 5.30 Round House Gallery
(ends 23 March)
The International Connection

12 – 8 ICA Concourse & Foyer
(ends 16 March)
. . . No Country for Old Men

12 – 8 ICA Main Gallery
(ends 16 March)
Without the Walls

12 – 8 ICA New Gallery
(ends 16 March)
West of West

8.00 Royal Court Theatre
The Liberty Suit: Project Co
(ends)

9.00 Sugawn Folk Kitchen
Traditional Music Session

Venues

Action Space
16 Chenies Street WC1
Tel 637 7664
Tube Goodge Street
Buses 14 24 29 73
Adm Exhibition Free
Performances £1 except
Friday & Saturday – £2 for
2 shows

Angela Flowers Gallery
11 Tottenham Mews
off Tottenham Street W1
Tel 637 3089
Tube Goodge Street
Buses 14 24 29 73
Adm Free

Annely Juda Fine Art
11 Tottenham Mews
off Tottenham Street W1
Tel 637 5517/8
Tube Goodge Street
Buses 14 24 29 73
Adm Free

Battersea Arts Centre
Lavender Hill SW11
Tel 223 9311
Train BR Clapham Junction
(3 minutes)
Buses 45 77 168 to door
19 37 39 49 249 to
Clapham Junction
Adm Exhibitions Free
Adm Concerts £1.10

The British Museum
Great Russell Street WC1
Tel 636 1555
Tubes Holborn, Russell Square,
Tottenham Court Road,
Booth Street
Buses 14 24 29 68 73 77
77A 77B 77C 170 188 239
Adm £1.40 Adults; OAPs,
Students, Children 70p
Pre booked school parties
70p.

Camden Centre
Euston Road NW1
Tube Euston Square
All buses to Euston Station
Adm £3 £2.50 £2 £1.50

Civic Hall Wimbledon
Queen's Road
Wimbledon SW19
Tube Wimbledon
Adm TBC

Crafts Council Gallery
12 Waterloo Place
Lr Regent Street SW1
Tel 839 1917/6306
Tube Piccadilly Circus
All Regent Street buses
Adm Free

52 Earlham Street Gallery
Earlham Street WC2
Tubes Leicester Square,
Covent Garden
All Leicester Square,
Covent Garden buses
Adm Free

Fairfield Hall
Park Lane
Croydon
Tel 688 9291
BR Croydon
Adm £4 £3.50 £3 £2.50 £2

The Fine Art Society
148 New Bond Street Wi
Tel 629 5116
Tubes Green Park, Piccadilly
Circus, Oxford Circus,
Bond Street
All Bond Street buses
Adm Free

Gaumont State Kilburn
High Road
Kilburn NW6
Tel 624 8081
Tubes Kilburn High Road,
Kilburn
All Kilburn High Road buses
Adm £3 £2.50 £2 £1.50

Half Moon Theatre
27 Alie Street E1
Tel 480 6465
Tube Aldgate East
All buses to Aldgate East
Adm £1.50

ICA
Nash House
The Mall SW1
Tel 930 0493
Box Office 930 3647
Recorded Info 930 6393
Tube Embankment, Charing
Cross,
Piccadilly Circus
All buses to above
Adm Theatre £1; Cinema £1.50
Lectures 80p
Day Membership 30p

Irish Centre
52 Camden Square NW1
Tel 485 0051/2
Tube Camden Town
All buses to Camden Town
Adm TBC

Lyric Studio Theatre
King Street
Hammersmith W6
Tel 437 3686
Tube Hammersmith Central
Adm £2

National Book League
7 Albemarle Street W1
Tel 493 9001
Tube Green Park
Buses 9 14 22
Adm Free

National Film Theatre
South Bank SE1
Tel 928 3232 (Box)
928 3842/3 (Office)
Tube Waterloo
Buses 1A 4 68 171 176
Adm Reserved £1.20
Unreserved 90p

National Poetry Centre
21 Earls Court Square SW5
Tel 373 7861/2
Tube Earls Court
All Earls Court buses V
Admission 70p

The National Club
Kilburn High Road
London NW6
Tel 328 3141
Tubes Kilburn
All Kilburn buses
Adm £1

The Old Vic
Waterloo Road SE1
Tel 928 6111
Tube Waterloo
BR Waterloo
Buses 68A 501 502
All buses to Waterloo Depot
Adm Stalls £6 £5.50 £4.50
£3.75 £2.50
Dress Circle £2.50 £3.75
£5.50
Upper Circle £2.50
Gallery £1

Pentax Gallery
6 Vigo Street W1
Tel 437 7358
Tube: Piccadilly Circus
All buses to Rent Street
Adm Free

Photographers' Gallery
8 Great Newport Street WC2
Tel 836 7860
Tube Leicester Square
All Leicester Square buses
Adm Free

Poplar Civic Theatre
Bow Road
Poplar E3
Tube Bow Road
All Bow Road buses
Adm £3 £2.50 £2 £1.50

Queen Elizabeth Hall
South Bank Concert Halls SE1
Tel 928 3191 (Box)
Tube Waterloo, Embankment
Buses 1 4 68 70 76 149 168A
171 176 188 239 501 507
Adm £3.50 £2.60 £2.10 £1.60
£1

RCA Gallery
Royal College of Arts
Kensington Gore SW7
Tel 584 5020
Tubes South Kensington and
Kensington High Street
Buses 9 52 73
Adm Free

RIBA
66 Portland Place W1
580 5533
Tube Oxford Circus,
Warren Street
All buses to Oxford Circus
Adm Free

Ronnie Scott's
47 Frith Street W1
Tel 439 0747
Tubes Leicester Square
Piccadilly
All Leicester Square/
Piccadilly buses
Adm Mon to Thurs £5 (non-
member); £4 (member)
Fri & Sat £6 (non-
member); £5 (member)

Round House
Chalk Farm Road NW1
Tel 267 2541
Tube Chalk Farm
Buses 24 31 68
Adm Lectures £1 (50p
students, OAPs)
Evening Events £2.50 £2
Season Ticket for all lectures,
events £15 (on sale in
January only)
Gallery Free

Royal Albert Hall
Kensington Gore SW7
Tel 589 8212
Tube Kensington High Street
Buses 27 49 52 88
Adm £4 £3.50 £3 £2.50 £2

Royal Court
Sloane Square SW1
Tel 730 5171
Tube Sloane Square
All Kings Road Sloane Square
buses
Adm Upstairs Mon, Tues £1.50
Wed. — Sat £2
Adm Main Theatre £4 £2.75
£1.50

Royal Festival Hall
South Bank Concert Halls SE1
Tel 928 3191 (box)
Tube Waterloo, Embankment
Buses 1 4 68 70 76 149 168A
171 176 188 239 501 507
Adm Festival Hall £5
£4.25 £3.50 £2.75 £2 £1.20

Sadlers Wells Theatre
Rosebery Avenue EC1
Tel 278 6563
Tube Covent Garden
All Covent Garden Buses
Adm Stalls £5.75 £5 £4 £3.25
Dress Circle £5.75 £5
Upper Circle £2.50 £1.75 £1

S. East Gallery
5 New Church Road SE5
Tel 701 9152
Tube Elephant and Castle then
bus 12 35 45 68 171 176
Adm Free

St. John's
Smith Square SW1
Tel 222 1061
Tube Westminster
Buses 3 77 77A 159 168
to Millbank 10 149
507 stopping Horseferry
Rd. 88 to Marsham St.
Adm £3.50 £2.75 £2 £1.25
(unreserved)

Somerset House
Strand WC2
Tel 438 6332
Tube Embankment Charing
Cross Aldwych (Peak Hrs Only)
Buses 1 6 9 11 15
Adm 50p 75p £1

Sugawn Theatre and Folk
Kitchen
Duke of Wellington
Balls Pond Road N1
Tel 254 1458
Tubes Highbury & Islington
Adm Theatre £1.50
Sessions Free

Swiss Cottage Library
Avenue Road NW3
Tube Swiss Cottage
All Swiss Cottage buses
Adm Free

The Venue
160/162 Victoria Street SW1
Tel 834 5500
Tube & BR Victoria
All Victoria Street buses
Adm £3

Theo Waddington
25 Cork Street W1
Tel 734 3534
Tubes Green Park,
Piccadilly Circus
Buses 19 22 73 137
Adm Free

Watford Town Hall
Watford Herts
Tel Watford 26400
BR Watford Junction
Watford High Street
Green Line buses 708 719
Adm £3 £2.50 £2 £1.50

Wembley Conference Centre
Wembley, Middx
Tel 902 1234 (Box)
Tube Wembley Park, Wembley
Central
BR Wembley Central, Wembley
Complex
Buses 83 92 182
Adm TBC

Wigmore Hall
36 Wigmore Street W1
Tel 935 2141
Tube Bond St, Oxford Circus
All Oxford St Buses
Adm £2.50 £2 £1.50 £1
20% reduction when
booking for all 6 concerts

The Workshop
83 Conduit Street W1
Tel 242 5335
Tube Holborn, Russell Square
Adm TBC

*Bush Theatre
Shepherds Bush Green W12
Tel 743 3388
Tubes Shepherds Bush,
Goldhawk Road
Buses 12 49 88 105 137 220
295

*Riverside Theatre
Crisp Road
Hammersmith W6
Tube Hammersmith
Buses 9 11 27 33 220 265

*Check with venue for details

All information in this catalogue
is, to the best of our knowledge,
correct at time of going to press.
However, we accept no
responsibility for changes, and
strongly recommend festival-
goers to check with specific
venues prior to event, or to
consult newspaper classified
ads.

Charles would prefer to keep the jewellery in the safe.
But that would be like hiding the Waterford.

Ogham is an ancient form of Irish usually inscribed on standing stones and found throughout the Irish countryside. This example reads: AIB

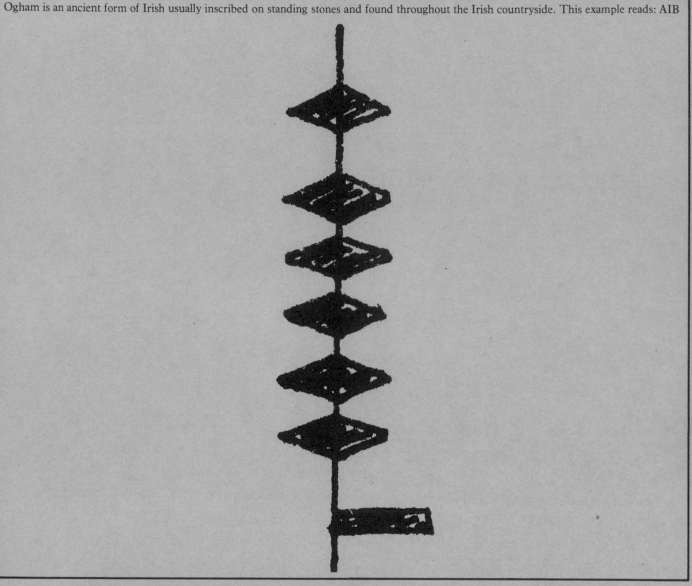

The language of banking is the language of understanding

Complete understanding of your banking needs.
That's what you can expect at Allied Irish Banks, Ireland's biggest bank in Britain, offering through its network full banking services to private and corporate business.
In addition, its Merchant Bank and Industrial Bank subsidiaries are fully operational in Britain.
Allied Irish Banks International Offices include New York, Chicago and Brussels.

Allied Irish Banks
Ireland's biggest bank in Britain

Head Office Britain: 64/66 Coleman Street, London EC2R 5AL. Tel: 01-588 0691.
British Branches: Birkenhead, Birmingham, Bristol, Cardiff, Coventry, Glasgow, Leeds, Leicester, Liverpool, London, Manchester, Nottingham, Watford and Wolverhampton.
Group Headquarters Dublin: Bankcentre, Dublin 4.

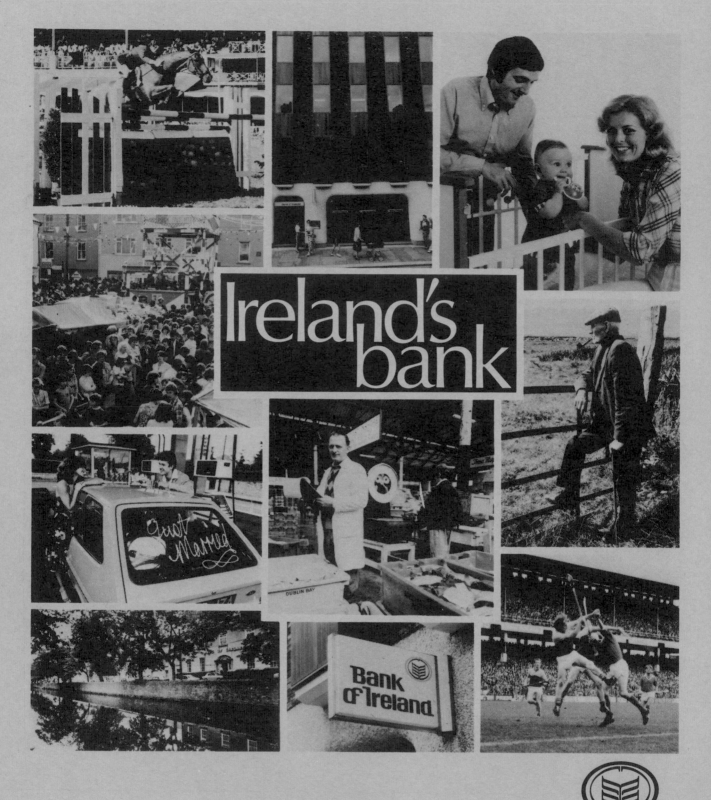

Ireland's
bank

Bank of Ireland
The bank of a lifetime

Republic of Ireland, the most profitable industrial location in Europe.

US Department of Commerce statistics for the period '74-'78 show a 29.9% average annual return on investment for US manufacturers located in the Republic of Ireland – more than twice the European average.

IDA Ireland
INDUSTRIAL DEVELOPMENT AUTHORITY

The Irish government's industrial development agency has offices in
London at 58 Davies St., London W1Y 1LB.
Telephone 01-629 5941.

FOR OUR 16-PAGE
FULL-COLOUR VERSION,
JUST FILL IN THE COUPON.

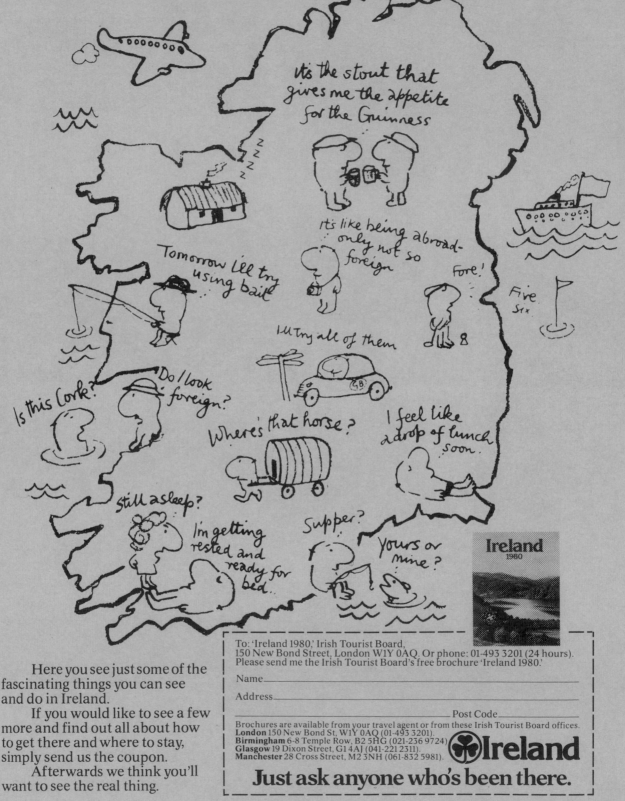

Here you see just some of the fascinating things you can see and do in Ireland.

If you would like to see a few more and find out all about how to get there and where to stay, simply send us the coupon.

Afterwards we think you'll want to see the real thing.

To: 'Ireland 1980,' Irish Tourist Board,
150 New Bond Street, London W1Y 0AQ. Or phone: 01-493 3201 (24 hours).
Please send me the Irish Tourist Board's free brochure 'Ireland 1980.'

Name

Address

Post Code

Brochures are available from your travel agent or from these Irish Tourist Board offices.
London 150 New Bond St, W1Y 0AQ (01-493 3201).
Birmingham 6-8 Temple Row, B2 5HG (021-236 9724)
Glasgow 19 Dixon Street, G1 4AJ (041-221 2311).
Manchester 28 Cross Street, M2 3NH (061-832 5981).

Ireland

Just ask anyone who's been there.

DM1   DM1

All things considered, is it so remarkable that Ireland also runs a rather enjoyable airline?
Aer Lingus ☘

Fourteen years ago an idea
became reality: a centre in
which designers of many
disciplines could work
together to stimulate the
highest standards of quality
and workmanship in Irish
industry.

In the cathedral city of
Kilkenny that reality has
flourished and already
wields an influence far
beyond Ireland.

On international frontiers
of good design for consumer,
industrial and craft products
this name will be increasingly
heard in the coming decade.

Kilkenny

Kilkenny Design Workshops
Kilkenny, Ireland
telephone Kilkenny 22118
telex Ireland 8727

A SENSE OF LEP

Lep Ireland is rather like the tip of an iceberg.
There is much more to us than meets the eye.

The Lep Organisation is a world-wide Group of
Companies engaged in all forms of international
transport and allied services.

One of the Lep specialist services is the Fine Arts
Department at the John F. Kennedy Estate in Dublin.

The Department is proud to be associated with this
major Festival of the Irish Arts in London. The
services provided by Lep for a Sense of Ireland include
the skilled packing and handling of a vast array of
valuable and unique exhibits as well as a comprehensive
range of freight forwarding services including
documentation for customs requirements.

So, when you next think about Lep, it makes sense to
think of us as a highly personalised resourceful unit.

John F. Kennedy Estate, Dublin 12.
Telephone 501020. Telex: 4356.

Lep (Ireland) Ltd.,

Rail freight: coping with the massive transport needs of heavy industry.

Streamlined bus services in Ireland's cities, now made more efficient with Europe's most up-to-date control systems.

Road freight gives industry a fast and flexible haulage system.

Air conditioned coaches on Mainline Rail with first class food available on most routes.

Expressway. A new standard of road travel that covers the country.

Rapid Transit System. A look towards the future role of urban transport.

CIE

TURNING THE WHEELS OF PROGRESS IN IRELAND'S FAVOUR